Baseball Family is b
lically-based inform₂
hancing your relationships. This book is timely and important
for living life to its fullest and building community the right
way. Truly, it's a must-read!

—Michelle Medlock Adams, Award-winning author of
more than 100 books, including: *Love Connects Us All*
and *Our God is Bigger Than That!*

I love this book! *Baseball Family: The 9 Core Qualities of
Loving Relationships* is a grand slam! Whether you need to
connect with your community, friends, or family, this book
needs to be the cleanup hitter in your daily lineup of personal readings.

—Del Duduit, Bestselling author of *Dugout Devotions,*
sportswriter, and broadcaster

Baseball Family is a heartfelt guide on how to genuinely love
people. The book is filled with real-life experiences that will
make you laugh and cry, all while you learn how to foster
rock-solid, God-honoring relationships.

—Tony Beltran, National Director of Compassion
International Dominican Republic

Do you struggle with a longing for connection but are unsure how to search for it and find it? Billie has written a book
just for you detailing the nine core qualities of loving others
and how that can impact your desire for connection and relationships. I am so grateful to have this resource and offer it
to others.

—Jennifer Hand, MAPC, author of *My Yes is on the
Table* and Executive Director of Coming Alive Ministries

If you long to build deeper, more meaningful relationships, read this book. Billie Jauss reveals a wealth of wise, practical, and biblical information on how to connect with people at far more than a surface level.

—Carol Kent, Executive Director of Speak Up Ministries, Speaker and Author, *Speak Up with Confidence* (NavPress)

Baseball Family is a well-written guide, making it easy to understand and follow! This book will benefit every person who reads it from college students to seasoned adults! You will feel empowered to implement the strategies given from start to finish!

—Caris Snider-Best-Selling Author, Speaker, Podcaster, & Certified Life Coach

Billie Jauss turns a double play with *Baseball Family:* not only does she provide an essential guide for navigating relationships in the world of sports, but also a helpful discipleship tool for anyone who wants to engage others in a more Christ-like way.

—Rev. Dr. Trent Casto, Senior Pastor of Covenant Church of Naples and author of *2 Corinthians: God's Strength in Our Weakness*

Baseball Family isn't just about baseball; it's about life's ever-changing landscapes and the opportunities that come with it. Whether you are a baseball enthusiast or someone who has experienced relocating to new places, making friends, and navigating different stages of life, This is a must-read for anyone in need of a reset!

—Dr. Jen Bennett, Entrepreneurship Professor, Host of *She | Impacts Culture Podcast*

If you want a road map for building, developing, and fostering meaningful relationships that center around nine core qualities, *Baseball Family* is the book for you!

—Michelle Watson Canfield, PhD, LPC, Author, *Let's Talk: Conversation Starters for Dads and Daughters*, Podcast host, *The Dad Whisperer*

Miscommunication is one of the biggest contributors to relationship difficulties. But we can learn healthier rules of engagement with others. Billie Jauss shares in *Baseball Family* her real-life examples with implementable strategies to improve your relationships.

—Dr. Michelle Bengtson Board Certified Clinical Neuropsychologist, award-winning podcast host, and author

BASEBALL FAMILY

NINE CORE QUALITIES FOR DEVELOPING

HEALTHY RELATIONSHIPS

BILLIE JAUSS

END GAME
Press

End Game Press books may be purchased in bulk at special discounts
for sales promotion, corporate gifts, ministry, fund-raising, or
educational purposes. Special editions can also be created to
specifications. For details, contact Special Sales Dept., End Game
Press, P.O. Box 206, Nesbit, MS 38651 or info@endgamepress.com.

Visit our website at www.endgamepress.com.

Library of Congress Control Number: 2023951936
HB: 9781637971994
PB ISBN: 9781637971321
eBook ISBN: 9781637972014

Cover by Dan Pitts
Interior Design by Typewriter Creative Co.

Printed in the United States of America
10 9 8 7 6 5 4 3 2 1

Dedication

My Baseball Family

For over 35 years, you've loved me well.
You've taught me how to continue
to share the qualities needed to love those
we encounter each baseball season.
May that legacy of love continue for many more.

Contents

★ ★ ★

THE FOUNDATIONS OF
FOUR RELATIONSHIPS

I didn't choose this lifestyle. I was thrown into it when my husband took a job in professional baseball. It took time to acclimate.

My husband, David, is a professional baseball coach, and I've learned to embrace the experiences and continue to live life to the fullest with each new season.

Throughout the years in professional baseball, I've found we have four types of relationships. We begin with *Accidental Acquaintances,* which can grow into *Social Circles* or even connect as *Kindred Spirits.* Then the very few become *Forever Family.*

We can enter each relationship with intentionality, a determination to do what God wants us to do within those moments, months, or years.

I've found myself among people and cultures where I felt uncomfortable. Adventuring into new places, I sometimes roamed into wrong behaviors and attitudes. But I learned a better way.

Learning how to encourage building community with

people was built on embracing these four types we encounter. Being able to discern the four groups helps me to nurture the unique communities I find myself in each baseball season.

The Mission Field

Baseball is where God has placed us. David and I know baseball is our mission field. Not only has David had a career in baseball, but I've dedicated my time to the women of baseball.

Over the years, we've lived in Wilson, NC; West Palm Beach, FL; Harrisburg, PA; Chicago; Boston; Ft. Myers, FL; Los Angeles; Vero Beach, FL; Baltimore; Sarasota and Ft. Lauderdale, FL; New York City; Port St. Lucie, FL; Pittsburgh; Bradenton, Anna Maria Island, FL, and Naples, FL. in the United States. We've also lived in Venezuela and the Dominican Republic.

Our goal is to develop loving relationships wherever God has placed us and with whomever He puts in our path. Loving one another is a command, not a feeling.

A Life of Upheaval

Of the four most popular professional sports in the USA— football, basketball, baseball, and hockey—the average player stays with a team for only three to five years. Within baseball, even if a player remains with the same team, they may shift back and forth from major to minor leagues while still in the same organization.

The season starts with six weeks of spring training, then off to the town where they will play during the summer. The potential of playing in winter ball—the baseball season in the Dominican Republic, Puerto Rico, Venezuela, Mexico, or Colombia—can be another temporary move that fills some with excitement and others with angst.

Each of those moves likely means a short-term relocation

for the family. They also have a move to their off-season home for the four-month off-season.

In the frequency of upheaval, we can only live our healthiest and best selves if we break down the walls that hold us back by stepping out in faith. Those who have committed to trusting God have a distinct advantage in times of uncertainty—even in relationships.

My baseball family is not my family of origin, but they have helped me become the woman Christ created me to be. I've learned more about the dynamics of loving one another than I ever learned from my birth family.

Life Scenarios

In the baseball world, we don't get to choose the friends we spend time with during the season. They come with the team. Still, we build and nurture a community and relationships. Navigating the different connections with others is challenging.

Many of you reading haven't lived the experience of baseball life, but I'm sure some have experienced moving to a new city and having new neighbors. We get a new job and have an entirely new group to get to know.

We encounter people while shopping for groceries, waiting at the dealership for a car repair, traveling, at church, or out at dinner.

As our kids enter school, we find ourselves in another group of moms. They begin to play sports, join clubs, or theater—another group of new acquaintances. Having a new baby throws us into groups of new connections with families who also have children.

Empty nesters, military families who move every few years—even missionaries—are in new countries and different cultures. All of these people experience a new group of potential friends.

I've experienced many of these scenarios in baseball, with kids, and now as an empty nester. I learned lessons, along with the ups and downs of navigating relationships.

Just as Jesus had acquaintances who did not become His close confidantes, we will also encounter many people just briefly. But just like Jesus, we will have acquaintances who become as close as the disciples did to Him.

As we meet new people, our connections either remain topical or grow. Some grow at warp speed—and we don't remember when we didn't know each other—while others never deepen.

In every chance meeting or deep relationship, we are called to love. Our love comes in abundance from God. Use that supply to pour out onto the lives of the people you encounter.

A New Command

"A new command I give you: Love one another.
As I have loved you, so you must love one another.
By this everyone will know that you are my disciples
if you love one another."

John 13:34-35

The family of God was on the precipice of a horrible loss. They weren't sure Jesus would rise and come again. Hadn't He been the core of their connectedness?

Jesus gave the disciples the new command to love one another just before ascending to God in heaven. He says others will know we are His disciples by how we love them.

Loving one another is the central focus of Jesus' earthly ministry. First, with God, which He made possible for us. Then with others. Jesus calls us to love one another.

Biblical love is the decision to compassionately, responsibly, and righteously pursue the well-being of others. It's not just liking someone.

Loving means connecting on a deeper level and seeking the best of others, even though we may not feel like doing so. Love is more than warm feelings. Love reveals itself in action. The world thinks that love is what makes a person feel good and we should compromise our moral principles and others' rights to obtain that love.

Sometimes it doesn't always feel good when we are called to love others. And at all times, we are to hold firm to our values while loving the unlovable.

Everyone believes love is important. The majority of society thinks of love as a feeling. Love is a choice and an action—true Christian faith results in loving behavior.

God is our source. He loved us enough to sacrifice His Son for the forgiveness of our sins. John says God is love, not that love is God. Our world has turned these two concepts around.

Jesus is our example of love. Everything He did in life and earth was supreme love. The Holy Spirit gives us the power to love. He lives in our hearts and makes us more and more like Christ.

The Four Relationships

God's love always involves a choice and an action. We learn the application as we navigate the four relationships we have in our lives: *Accidental Acquaintances, Social Circles, Kindred Spirits,* and *Forever Family.*

Nine players occupy the baseball field and have dynamic relationships and position-specific intentional qualities they bring to the game. Their connections represent the four types of relationships introduced in *Baseball Family.*

Accidental Acquaintances

The first type of friend is an *Accidental Acquaintance.* On the baseball field, the first and third basemen represent this connection.

Positionally, they are on the corners of the infield, not at the center of the baseball diamond nor in the midst of most plays. They are not in direct communication with more than one other player. Being on the outskirts of the interactions, they are not involved in plays together.

In our daily relationships, these may be the people we meet in passing, on a plane, at a meeting, or an event. We may follow each other on social media and like pictures when we see them. This group can be a large number of people. On Facebook, our profile caps the amount to five thousand friends. Instagram is limitless, it seems.

Our connection can stay respectful and loving by our being friendly and nonconfrontational, even if we disagree in our beliefs. It takes commitment to find out more about them and love them anyway.

Accidental Acquaintances can grow, but the friends that stay at this level do not evolve into deep connections. In my baseball family, these are the concession workers, ticket takers, ushers, and others we meet in passing.

Social Circle

In the *Social Circle*, the outfielders represent these relationships. There are three outfielders—the right fielder, the center fielder, and the left fielder. They are positioned from right to left when viewed from home plate. The right and left fielders are considered corner outfielders.

The center fielder is the captain of the outfield, taking precedence over the corner outfielders if they attempt to field the same ball. The center fielder will yell, "I got it!" to call off the other outfielders when they are also trying to catch the fly ball.

The outfielders are far apart but must constantly communicate and work together. They have similar skills and practice all things together. The other positions each have specific responsibilities and aspects of the game that are particular to their positions.

Our *Social Circle* may be the people we meet at Bible study, go to church with, are in a small group with, or serve in a charitable organization with. Most of these friends are in the same parenting, work, or marriage season. These friendships are usually based on like-mindedness.

When a luncheon with a large group is happening at our house, we invite them. We value them and want to include them in our events and parties. We invite their kids to our children's birthday parties.

We know a little about their lives and have personal contact by text or email. An occasional lunch may occur to discuss pertinent matters concerning an event or social celebration. The relationship is recognized but topical. It isn't deeper than a drive-by experience.

Social Circles are a smaller group than *Accidental Acquaintances*. Growth in these relationships occurs when there is a deeper desire to know the person. A connection of interest and acceptance is felt between them.

In my baseball life, the people working at the ballpark whom I see every home game, and many of the wives and girlfriends of the front office staff, fall in this group. Even some players' and coaches' wives and girlfriends stay in my *Social Circle*.

Kindred Spirit

The third level of friends is *Kindred Spirit*. The second baseman and the shortstop, the middle infielders, represent these relationships. They both cover the middle of the infield, the heart of the diamond. (The baseball field is the shape of a diamond.)

They are the double-play combo, combining efforts to get two outs. Communication is the heart of the duo during defensive plays, relaying information to all players, including the pitcher. They are the captains of defense.

They are the heart of the defense and are involved in almost every defensive strategy, from hits to runners on base, both before the pitch is made and when balls are hit.

They are responsible for everything when the ball is in play and with runners on base. Their communication is vital to having all players in the right spot and executing the fundamentals to limit the opponent from scoring.

Kindred Spirits get us. They understand what matters and respect our beliefs. We realize what makes them tick. We share a mutual respect for what breaks each other's hearts. We encourage one another to soar where God has placed us.

There's time to listen when a *Kindred Spirit* calls with a burning issue. We have the intuition to step back when we need to be moving forward. We celebrate their victories and cry over their defeats. We are their biggest cheerleaders but correct them when their paths stray.

The door is open to our homes, even if unfolded clothes lie on the couch and yesterday's dishes are in the sink. We don't apologize when our kids act out of sorts.

Our hair can be three-days-old, oily, and in a bun again. Today's t-shirt from yesterday with baby puke stains, mac and cheese on our yoga pants—and we still let them in. Being *Kindred Spirits* is a beautiful friendship. We love one another as Christ loves us.

One of the reasons a *Kindred Spirit* relationship may not grow to the next level is proximity. We are only in the same city for six months in baseball. If we get fired, released, or traded, we may never be in the same vicinity again. Our relationship is still very close, and our memories are sweet, but contact is not as consistent.

Growth is stifled when an offense breaks trust. Sometimes misunderstandings happen, and our relationships sever.

You are still at a deeper level than a social sister, but don't go forward. Progression into the next level of friendship happens naturally. Trust grows more profound, and love grows stronger. The transition isn't always apparent. We just know when it happens.

Many of my friends in baseball didn't start as *Kindred Spirits*. Some were not so friendly. And others I didn't want to spend time getting to know. We may like someone a lot but don't feel a deeper connection.

The wives and girlfriends of players and coaches come from different cultures, beliefs, and morals. I love every one of them, but sometimes there's that special one I connect with on a deeper level.

Forever Family

The last type of friendship is the *Forever Family*. The players that relate to this level are the pitcher and catcher. The batterymates have to make it happen.

They partner up when facing each batter at the plate. Not needing anyone else to strike out a hitter strengthens their connection.

However, if a player gets on base, the catcher has the pitcher's back by trying to throw out the baserunner.

The starting pitcher establishes the momentum of each game. He is the center of responsibility. Communication between the pitcher and the catcher is essential. Trust between the two is necessary.

Game plans are established before they hit the field. Their strategy continues throughout the game, from relaying each sign before a pitch is made to mound visits and in-between innings talks.

The link between batterymates is the same from Little

League to the Majors. Their relationship is closer than other players on the field.

Forever Family relationships are incredibly close and trusted friends. They're the ones we pour our hearts out to when we need to vent, knowing they will not judge us or condemn us. They stop everything to rescue us, bringing our favorite junk food and picking the perfect movie.

When we have our babies, they take our other kids to give mom a bit of time with the baby alone. They clean our houses without asking and boss our kids around like they are their own. Our spouse feels like the *Forever Family* friend, somewhat like a sister, is part of the family.

When we need Jesus in skin, they are there at the drop of a hat. They hit their knees and cry out to Jesus for us. They don't just say, "I'll pray for you." They start before we finish our request.

These friends are our *Kindred Spirits,* taken to a new level of commitment and loyalty. They love us fiercely. A change in our attitude smells like a fire to them—not just a question of the smell of smoke—and they set us straight.

We will have our friends that betray our trust. When we are family forever, it cuts us to the core, but they are family. It doesn't mean we allow hurtful actions. We tend to forgive the damages and give them a second chance. We don't give up on each other.

Our *Forever Family* grows together, sometimes one more than the other. When one of us is slipping, the other lends a hand. Encouragement overflows. We challenge each other to be better people.

My *Forever Family* in baseball is a short list. Our connection is profound. We stay connected even when we are in a different city or team. They know when I need them, and they show up or send things that cheer me up.

Not everyone we encounter becomes *Forever Family,*

and sometimes people we meet never even enter our *Social Circle*. Crazy as it can sometimes feel, challenging as it often is, a life immersed in baseball has taught me that developing solid and sustainable relationships is possible. It's a pattern that parallels what the Bible teaches. We have a command to love one another and love them like Jesus.

Loving like Jesus is hard to do. When we bicker, are jealous, or react rather than respond, our actions do not show the love of Christ. Comparison and fear stifle our spirits from being open to accepting the love of others. That's not how Jesus operated and not what He expects from us.

Making Connections

Relationship obstacles started early in our baseball career. Dragging baggage from the experiences of previously failed friendships didn't help. I had to learn to discern the different relationships and nurture each.

David stepped into his dream of being a professional baseball coach from college ball. I was launched into a new and intriguing life with the possibility of new friends in a new place.

Entering our first spring training, I had high hopes and an open mind. Probably a bit naïve about how things worked in baseball, but I was excited to find my people.

Connecting with others was more complicated than I imagined. My exuberant youthful personality annoyed some seasoned wives, while others found me refreshing.

"The adults are talking," a fellow baseball wife responded when I tried to include myself in a conversation. The other wives in the group were baseball veterans, so I, the rookie, was an easy target. They giggled and stared.

I thought we were in this baseball thing together as wives. I'd hoped we'd all be friends. The interaction ripped out my heart. I retreated to a corner alone, wanting nothing to do with this "family."

A few weeks later, a fellow baseball wife, Renette, invited us to their home. As we were leaving, she gathered her family and prayed over us.

She leaned where God called and took a risk to pray for an unbelieving young girl and her husband at the beginning of what was to be a long career in baseball. Renette has been one of my closest mentors over the years.

What if she hadn't reached out? What if she hadn't taken a risk with a naïve, exuberant young baseball wife who was going about relationships all wrong?

Being an example of love and loving one another is the foundation for developing relationships wherever God has placed us—and with the types of relationships He puts in front of us.

Moving Forward

I've failed, been disappointed by others, and been loved beyond measure since Renette prayed over and for us. I wouldn't trade my baseball family for anything in the world. They've guided me to become a more loving person to everyone.

All the experiences, positive and negative, challenged me. I began to take ownership of my emotions, to discern the different connections, and to learn the characteristics required to build community. It made all the difference for me. And it can for you too.

I'm confident you can gain knowledge from the lessons I've learned in baseball. Be assured that there is no need to understand the game of baseball to gain from these helpful examples. I'll explain things along the way.

I pray I can help you find your footing where God has placed you. My desire is to help you glean from my baseball life's experiences so that your relationships will be better, stronger— rock solid.

We can love others with grace when we love like Jesus using the Starting Nine Core Qualities.

We will implement the qualities within each relationship as we move into the qualities. As we sincerely seek to understand and integrate these principles into our lives, I am convinced we will take responsibility for how we foster relationships.

As we learn together, I pray we build fruitful relationships with the guidance of these lessons. The work is not easy, but it will be worth the investment and the risk. I am so excited to get started.

THE STARTING NINE CORE QUALITIES

The four types of relationships—*Accidental Acquaintances, Social Circles, Kindred Spirits,* and *Forever Family*—are solidified by learning the Starting Nine Core Qualities needed to love others. The qualities are...

- Selflessness: seeing others' needs as more important than our wants.
- Inclusion: going above and beyond to build connections with people we might never choose.
- Supportive: helping others along the way with God's word and prayer.
- Peacemaker: using God's love to create loving relationships even when chaos reigns.
- Encouraging: helping stimulate confidence and hope by putting courage in another person's spirit.
- Compassionate: showing sympathy toward another's distress while having the desire to alleviate their pain.
- Respectful: caring enough about another person to consider how our actions impact them.

- Trustworthy: pouring out dependable, reliable, and honest character.

- Generous: giving more affection and tenderness than is necessary.

Discovering these virtues and how they develop in our network of loving relationships with people we may or may not choose frees us to build a community of love.

The personal qualities necessary to foster healthy relationships became a requirement for me. I found that the Starting Nine Core Qualities help support the foundation of building mutually beneficial interactions in and out of baseball life.

Two teams take the field in a baseball game. Each has a starting lineup of nine players who together work for the best potential outcome in the game. The starting nine players are essential to their success.

I believe the Starting Nine Core Qualities are indispensable in cultivating an intentional Christian life:

- Making connections,

- Building a community,

- Encouraging one another,

- All while loving others.

For too many years, I tried to chameleon to each new group I entered. Trying to be what others wanted me to be didn't help me have successful connections. I wasn't concerned if others were receiving care from me.

I grew angry if someone didn't size up to how I thought they should respond to my attempt to fit in.

One baseball season, I met a wife I thought could be a dear friend. We would sit together during games and talk about our kids and husbands, but fast-forward a few weeks. I walked into the stadium family room to a group of women staring and snickering, including my "friend." They immediately stood and left the family room.

I was devastated. The roller coaster of thoughts flew through my head. What had I done? Was I wearing the wrong outfit? Did my kids do something mean to their kids? Had my husband been rude to a husband?

It was none of the above. My "friend" tried to fit into their group and used my oversharing to be included in the mean-girl, popular group.

I quickly learned that morphing myself into what others should like wasn't honoring who God had created me to be.

We are unique individuals. Changing who we are to be liked and build relationships fails every time.

I had to find a better way to cultivate loving environments because that didn't work. I began to delve into scripture to see what Jesus said. It wasn't as much what He said but how He lived it out.

In baseball, I've learned how to encourage building community with a group in a one-of-a-kind situation in a specific place at a particular time that previously left me frustrated and lonely.

I pray that my experiences will encourage you to step out and live the Nine Core Qualities to love others.

Part of the Family

"For this reason I kneel before the Father,
from whom every family in heaven
and on earth derives its name.
I pray that out of his glorious riches
he may strengthen you with power through
his Spirit in your inner being,
so that Christ may dwell in
your hearts through faith.

And I pray that you,
being rooted and established in love,
may have power, together with
all the Lord's holy people,
to grasp how wide and long
and high and deep is the love of Christ,
and to know this love that surpasses knowledge
—that you may be filled to the measure
of all the fullness of God."

Ephesians 3:14-19

The family of God includes all who believe in Him, past, present, and future. We are all part of the family because we have the same Father.

God is the source of all creation, all people included. He promises His love and power to all of His family. God's love is wide. It reaches every cranny of our experience. It covers the width of our experience and reaches out to the entire world.

So many times, I try to do things on my own. I'm incredibly independent and focused on accomplishing tasks. I can bulldoze my way with the best of them. Then I get frustrated when things don't work out.

God wants us to be strengthened in our spirits by His Holy Spirit. We don't need to change our situation or the work we do. We need to change internally. When we rely on Jesus for our strength, the outcome becomes the product of His glory. His glorious riches.

We have power together. We have that power through Jesus' love for us, through His Holy Spirit. God's love is long, continuing throughout our entire lives, even into death.

It is high, as it rises to the heights of celebrations. God's love is deep, reaching into the depths of discouragement, despair, and death.

The source of God's love extends to us and others. We extend it to others by embracing the qualities that nurture relationships.

The fullness of God is expressed in Christ. We are complete when we are in a relationship with Christ and filled with His Holy Spirit. In that fullness, we can pour God's love into others—whether they are *Accidental Acquaintances, Social Circles, Kindred Spirits,* or *Forever Family.*

No matter the growth, the core qualities of selflessness, inclusion, support, peacemaking, encouragement, compassion, respect, trustworthiness, and generosity will help us present the love of Christ. God has come to save us. Trust Him in all situations; there's no reason to fear. He strengthens us to stand firm. We have victory in Him.

As we dig into the virtues, we learn to fulfill God's command to love one another. To discern and grow in our four types of relationships. Let's not become people of success but instead try to become people spreading Christ's love.

I'm praying for you and for all the Lord will reveal to us.

STARTING NINE CORE QUALITY #1

Selflessness

The word *selfless* overwhelms me with the feeling that I will be neglected. Selfish thought, I know, but with past experiences, I've been taken advantage of and my feelings ignored.

Selflessness is the opposite of selfishness. Selfless love means seeing others' needs as more important than our wants. Growing love toward others starts with you.

Many of us were taught to place others first. Unfortunately, this doesn't come naturally. The selfless quality goes against human nature. Our culture tells us to put ourselves first, which is countercultural to what Jesus teaches us.

Baseball Hierarchy

Anger and the need for revenge filled me when a dear friend hurt me deeply. Another baseball wife whom I had grown close to over the season. Our kids were the same age, and we spent a lot of time at the ballpark and the neighborhood park when the team was away.

We took turns keeping each other's kids when we had a night off. I loved having little girls—she was terrified by three boys. She was a player's wife. In our early years in baseball, I was the age of the players' wives. I became friends with many, but this girl was special.

I shared a lot of deep thoughts with her. We cried over hurts, celebrated successes, and talked on the phone late into the night after the kids went to bed when the hubbies weren't home.

Then the playoffs came, and her husband didn't make the roster. For some reason, she blamed my husband for shunning hers. She said hurtful things and told secrets I'd shared with her to other wives. I was mortified and embarrassed.

She broke my heart and my trust. I was mad. I wanted her to hurt as badly as I hurt. I told anyone who would listen how she betrayed me. It became all about me and my pain, all at her expense. How could she cause such damage to our friendship?

The other wives and girlfriends on the team knew when to avoid conflict, and they did. As the playoffs ended, I was sitting alone, outraged and offended. I cringe to think about how I acted and pushed everyone away. I didn't have strong faith then and handled relationships terribly.

Every association was about my feelings, desires, and needs. Yes, my former friend acted immaturely and probably used our connection to get her husband in better standing with the coaching staff. But I would have treated her differently if I had the wisdom to love others. I was selfish.

For many years in baseball and life, I've wanted others to like me. Not because I was friendly, but because I "deserved" to be a part of every group. I was arrogant in believing they should include me. Many times, I wasn't invited to join whatever they were doing.

The baseball hierarchy places more significance on players than on coaches—the better the player, the more attention. If someone is in a higher pay grade, they get a higher degree of special treatment.

I felt like my husband should be treated the same. That was not the reality and is not to this day. I understand these players draw fans and sell tickets, but I saw how hard the coaches worked.

I got so caught up in me, me, me—that I lost sight of how much others need to be loved, not just seen as commodities.

I felt like I competed with everyone. At that time, I didn't think of others before myself. No one was taking care of me; why should I show love to them?

Our Responsibility

"It's not about you" is my favorite first line of any book, and I refer to it often. Reading that line shook me. The source was *The Purpose Driven Life* by Rick Warren.

Our life is much more than personal feelings. Before I committed my life to serving the Lord, I took everything personally. Encounters with mean people shook me to the core.

We encounter mean people each day. We aren't going to be clear of all pain from others. However, by surrendering our self-focus and leaning on Jesus, we open our hearts to love.

When the woman prayed over David and me at the beginning of our baseball career, we were rookies in the coaching world. Her husband previously played in the big leagues. His position was higher than my husband's.

The couple loved as Christ loves. Even though we were making poor social decisions, not following Christ, and were super young in the game, they embraced us. Seed planted.

The new friend's selfless behavior of praying for our baseball future spoke volumes about my immature spirit. I saw the light of Christ through their humility. Learning from a woman who was older than me and had lived a lot of life and learned plenty of lessons helped me to show that love to others.

Ten years into baseball, David and I recommitted our lives to serving the Lord. It took us a while for that seed to take root. We accepted Jesus as our Savior and left our desire to be our own saviors behind. Our experiences in friendship before Christ, compared to after following Christ, were drastically different.

We learned humility. Our desire to be more humble gave us tremendous opportunities to lean into the lives of others and to allow them into ours.

We cannot expect every person we come into contact with to return the love we spill out to them. However, we have a responsibility to love.

Taking Time

We've been blessed in baseball to build relationships with a diverse group of people, younger and older. Over the years, as David's and my faith grew, we saw how being considerate of others allowed for new friendships.

During spring training with the Red Sox, many of the staff stayed at the same hotel. As homeschoolers, our kids spent the entire spring in Florida. We encouraged them to spend time with people who worked with the team.

Many nights, one of the older couples, Johnny and Ruthie Pesky, sat by the pool after dinner. Johnny would smoke a cigar while Ruthie sat close by.

David and I loved listening to stories of the past. Johnny played for the Red Sox in 1942 before World War II and again from 1946 to 1952. He finished his career with the Tigers and the Senators.

My kids played in the pool, diving for rings or challenging each other with another swimming race when the couple showed up. I asked the kids to sit with us.

My request came with quite a few complaints from our sons. Selfishly being in the pool was much better than sitting with a bunch of older people, their parents included.

We listened to stories of "back in the day" baseball. Johnny offered exaggerated tales; Ruthie would call him out and interject her version. It was such a joyful time sitting in the presence of history.

The first few nights we'd sit together, our kids would be restless to return to their pool shenanigans. Then things changed. As they genuinely listened to the stories, they began to laugh when it was appropriate and ask questions when something needed clarifying.

One night, another coach called David and me over to meet his wife. He was new to the team, and we were excited to spend time getting to know them. I was surprised at how much time had passed while we were talking. I jumped up to check on the kids in the pool.

All three boys knew how to swim, there were other adults we knew by the pool, and we were only a few feet outside the fence, so I knew they were safe.

But the quiet is what startled me. The boys weren't in the pool when I peered over the fence. As I perused the deck, I smelled cigar smoke.

Following the smell of a cigar and swirls of smoke, I found Johnny and Ruthie sitting in their usual spot with the boys surrounding them. I turned back, excused myself from David and our new friends, and approached the boys. Their eyes were wide as they intently listened to the tale of the moment.

"Everything okay?" I asked as I slipped behind our youngest son. All three boys animatedly began talking all at once, telling me the latest tale.

The love in their eyes for the couple. The awe of the crazy baseball stories and banter. The boys' absolute joy glimmered in their eyes. They were sacrificing time in the pool to interact with people they hadn't wanted to spend time with before.

The boys shared later that sitting with them wasn't that bad. "Older people are actually interesting," one of the boys offered.

"Yeah, I like listening to what happened back in the day," another chimed.

Taking time from what we enjoy to spend time with someone we don't think is interesting often turns to delight. Turning over our defensiveness and focusing on Jesus' love for others allows us to love like Him. God will take care of us through it all.

• Hurts will happen.

• Pain will be inflicted.

• But He is with us to give us peace beyond all understanding.

The Driving Force

The first characteristic, selflessness, demands us to allow God to be the driving force in our relationships. Dying to self and focusing on the Lord's command is what we must do to help create an attitude of loving others.

Self-focused, we rely on our feelings to build or break connections. We cannot blame others. We need to look inside of us to find what needs to change. Healthy relationships begin with turning over defenses and focusing on Jesus' love for them.

God designed us to understand life together. Where two or more are together, He is with us. We cannot do life alone, nor can anyone else. We are a powerful force for the Lord together. Every part of the connection is essential to love one another.

Relationships are not all about you, but the process begins with you. Our connection with Jesus comes first. The more we follow God's word and deepen our love for Him, the more we become selfless.

Putting Him first and us second helps us to begin to see the need to open our hearts to receive the experiences God desires us to have.

Each of the four relationships benefits when we choose to put God first. *Accidental Acquaintances* feel loved when we show selfless love without expecting anything in return. *Social Circles* experience a sense of being seen when we take the time to notice their needs. *Kindred Spirits* experience understanding and acceptance. The *Forever Family* is the most reliable and opened up to mutual love.

Spiritual Unity

> *"Do nothing out of selfish ambition or vain conceit. Rather, in humility value others above yourselves,"*
>
> *Philippians 2:3*

If we go into new groups wanting to answer the question, What do I need?—we will fail to connect with the other person.

Selfish ambition makes us fail because others will never meet our expectations and needs. It causes quarrels and fights. When our selfish needs are unmet, we become angry and feel neglected.

An excessively high opinion of our appearance, abilities, or worth is the root of pride. Our vain conceit separates us from God and others; the glory of self before God is prideful. Pride does not come from God—it blinds us and separates us from His desire for us to love one another.

Pride can be reasonable self-respect, positive pride, or excessive self-esteem, acted out as arrogance or conceit. The Bible references the latter, more sinful meaning more frequently in the Old and New Testaments.

When we place the god of pride before an almighty God, it puts our needs and feelings above the needs of others. If we become comfortable with selfish ambition or vain conceit, we partner with pride, a spirit that will destroy any potential relationship.

The apostle Paul wrote Philippians while imprisoned. He expresses in the letter that true joy comes from Christ. He wants God's saints to live in the joy of the Lord instead of reacting to the circumstances around them.

Paul wrote some corrections to the Philippians. In chapter two, he instructs the church to have the mindset of Christ rather than conforming to others' ways of thinking.

The church in Philippi reflected great diversity. In this diversity, there were misunderstandings. In chapter four of Philippians, Paul addresses the division in the church and how their relational problems threaten their unity and joy.

Euodia and Syntyche, the two women at odds, had been workers for Christ in the church. Their broken relationship was massive because many had come to believe through their sharing. Paul urged them to resolve their conflict.

There will be division and arguments in response to our pride and unmet expectations, but to remain unreconciled should not occur. Seeking an attitude of selflessness and humility if a conflict is unresolved brings reconciliation.

Humble Examples

The opposite of pride is the virtue of humility. Selfish ambition is a form of the sin of pride.

Paul challenges the church in Philippi, and us, to imitate Christ's humility. Christ showed true humility when he became human. He laid aside His rights as God and poured out His life to pay the penalty we deserve. Laying aside self-interest is vital for all of our connections.

We must take Christ's attitude and love others while denying our recognition and what we think we deserve. When we give up selfish interests, we can pour out the love Christ calls us to give to others.

Jesus gives us His Holy Spirit to lead and guide our ability to lay down our personal needs and concerns. Utilizing His power gives us a selfless attitude. Finding joy in serving comes from imitating Jesus' humility.

Many people, even Christians, want to please themselves or live to have others like them. Selfish ambition is the opposite of serving the needs of others. Vain conceit is being excessively proud of or concerned about one's appearance, qualities, and achievements. Self-serving accolades cause friction.

Spiritual Unity

Paul stresses **spiritual unity**. He asks the Philippians to love one another and be one in spirit and purpose. We often measure greatness by looking at how we serve others—but not helping others without anything in return. We cannot bank on reciprocal affection and concern from others around us. Our foundation must be in Christ.

Building relationships takes a lot from us. Being filled with the love of Christ, the ultimate self-care, allows us to pour it out to others. Jesus is the best example of a servant, a vessel of love.

The word *nothing* in the scripture doesn't leave room for exceptions. We cannot choose to be selfish and not show love to the person we dislike for their flippant attitude. Deciding not to talk to the women God's placed in front of us because they aren't part of the crowd we want to be with. *If we are with her, the others may not want to hang with us.*

It would have been easier if Paul said we shouldn't do most things out of selfish ambition or conceit. "Most things" would give us an escape clause. *Nothing* requires a continual commitment to humble ourselves.

The prophet Daniel had excellent personal character. He is one of only a few in the Bible whom God doesn't say anything negative about his character. He shared the human nature of all other leaders in the Bible, but he seemed to rise above them because of his admirable qualities.

He displayed character by refusing to do wrong for foreign kings. Kings offered to pay him for his ability to interpret dreams, but he declined because he remained committed to God despite the pressure. He never lost his love for others, even in enemy cultures.

When King Nebuchadnezzar of Babylon, a foreign land to Daniel, desired a disturbing dream to be interpreted, the king summoned the magicians, enchanters, sorcerers, and astrologers (Daniel 2:1-28). When they could not analyze it, he ordered the execution of Babylon's wise men.

Daniel and his friends, Hananiah, Mishael, and Azariah (Shadrach, Meshach, and Abednego), had impressed the king a year earlier. The king found them ten times better than all the magicians and enchanters, so they entered his service.

The order to kill the wise men included Daniel and his friends. Daniel told the king he would interpret the dream for him.

Daniel returned home and shared the news with his friends. He urged them to plead for mercy from God. During the night, Daniel had a vision that revealed the mystery of the king's dream. Daniel shared it with him. Daniel gave all the glory to God, not his abilities.

King Nebuchadnezzar fell to the floor and worshiped Daniel. He then gave God the glory. The greatest king on earth was mad to confess the dominance of the true God. Daniel never lauded himself with the praise but continued to give it to God.

He asked the king not to kill all of the wise men of the kingdom. The king obliged and put Daniel in charge of all the wise men. He also remembered his friends, and they were promoted along with him. They would soon prove their faithfulness to God in the face of a deadly threat.

Not only did Daniel risk his life by interpreting for the king, but he also saved the lives of his many wise men. The magicians, enchanters, sorcerers, and astrologers were not his closest friends, and they didn't believe in God. Daniel did nothing out of selfish ambition or vain conceit.

He was wiser in the eyes of the king, but he didn't use that to gain power. He obeyed God and valued others above himself. God knows how to grant power to those who submit to His authority.

Throughout his long career, Daniel brought praise and honor to God through his faithfulness.

Selfless Humility

Even though being selfless is for the benefit of others, we can also gain from thinking of others first. When we show love to most people, they begin to reciprocate.

Selflessness seems more attainable as we learn from people in the Bible and how they lived in dysfunctional societies. My humanness wants to stop me from wanting to take care of myself and serve others. The pain of how I was treated. The feeling that I deserve more.

If anyone deserved more, it was Jesus while He was on earth. He existed in the form of God; however, He didn't use being equal to God for His gain. He gave up everything but His deity by taking on human flesh. He was selfless. He poured himself out fully to humanity. Jesus was entirely God and a complete man.

If we've gotten anything as followers of Christ, we should love others as Christ has loved us. Trying to push our way to the top or driving to get ahead of others never succeeds. Forget our needs long enough to value others.

Humility to many implies lowness in status rank or economic means. Here, we look at it as the opposite of importance or wealth. Culture sees humility as cowardly, whereas Christianity embraces a more powerful position.

We are to be submissive to God, modeling the characteristics of Christ. We choose a posture of humbleness. Jesus gave up His right to obey God and serve people.

Humility and love intimately intertwine through the gospel. Jesus showed both humility and love in all He did. Emulating Him in being selfless with one another develops stronger bonds.

Being humble and valuing others above ourselves is selflessness. If I am about me, I am selfish. If I'm about you, I am humble.

Humble examples are exemplified through our *Forever Family*. Spiritual unity deepens with *Kindred Spirits,* and *Social Circles* give us the opportunity to be humble examples. Each day, we can show *Accidental Acquaintances* they are valued.

Value above Ourselves

Creating an attitude of selflessness takes great personal strength and courage. We must commit to dying to ourselves, becoming others-focused, and stepping out confidently. We have an opportunity to make significant changes and begin to attract more people toward Jesus and us.

It's been challenging to write about selflessness. My natural condition is to take care of myself and to make excuses.

- I'm too busy.
- I don't want to deal with attitudes.
- I have enough connections to deal with more people.

I also feel like my selfishness sneaks in when I want to write this section my way, and God steps in and redirects where it's headed. Having to demonstrate selflessness is humbling. Changing our question from what we need or want to what God asks us to do, redirects our focus. Start with getting out of our heads. Our thoughts can keep us focused on ourselves. Begin to control the thoughts that keep us from appreciating others.

Not every person we meet will be *Forever Family*. However, to value others, we stay open to each person we meet, evaluating the interaction with an open heart. Each quality we learn can be applied to each type of friend, even if not reciprocated.

Accidental Acquaintances

The on-the-field comparison of the first and third basemen as *Accidental Acquaintances* exhibits selflessness in working together with the team, even though they are not in close contact.

Communication between them is rare. They are responsible for plays at their spot on the field with little connection with the rest of the defense. However, the greater good is their focus on participating as a group rather than an individual.

Accidental Acquaintance selfless behavior requires a smile when we meet, a like on social media, or a question about them.

Baseball summers are like repeating the same day over and over. Many of our game days in baseball are repetitive. We enter the ballpark through the same parking lot with the same attendants each game day. The same person mans the window where we pick up our tickets.

Most nights, we enter the same gate with our regular security staff. And the same with our family section and the ushers. Not all of the staff at the home ballparks are incredibly nice— some are even grumpy at times. But no matter how they act, I still pour out love to them.

The selfless things I've done are smiling, giving pats on the back, giving hugs, or asking if I can grab them a bottle of water. Humbling myself, not just rushing and not acknowledging them, takes a little time. Everyone welcomes time spent and, even more so, compliments.

The people in this category may be different, but thinking of how we can slow down and take a minute to show love to others allows us to act on the selfless quality. Learn to let go. Just do it without anything in return.

Social Circle

Outfielders represent the *Social Circle,* and their selflessness presents in their coverage of the entire outfield, backing up the infielders and trying to make sure no runs are scored when balls fall into play. They don't interact much, but they're there for the team.

With our *Social Circle,* we take time to make them feel seen. Sit beside them at Bible study. Hug them. Stop and talk when we see them. Invite them to group gatherings.

Begin to say yes to people we don't know very well. Putting our errands aside to spend time with them helps open opportunities to understand them better.

The baseball *Social Circle* is most of the wives, girlfriends, and family members that visit. We help each other with our kids, inviting them to tag along when going with my kids to grab a snack or walking to the family room.

When my kids were young, I would swap babysitting on off days. That way, we got at least a few date nights during the season.

We included family members when they visited, getting them where they needed to be and answering questions they might have.

One season, our oldest and middle sons were playing travel ball. A baseball wife offered to take our youngest to an away series. He loved not having to sit at his brothers' games, and I loved only having two to cart around.

We lived in the same apartment complex during that season. Each time we went to the pool, I texted the other wife and invited the kids, letting her have some time alone.

Kindred Spirit

The *Kindred Spirits* of the middle infielders demonstrate the ability to read each other's movements and step in front of or back each other up when needed.

They are the heart of the infield. To turn a double play, the players must coordinate steps without hesitation. The beat and flow, at best, are seamless.

Our selfless quality toward *Kindred Spirits* shows up in understanding and acceptance. Having the Christ-like attribute of humility and allowing them to share their hurts and hardships with us.

Being nonjudgmental and giving godly counsel without judgmental words strengthens the bond. Allowing them to share makes it not about us. It's about them during their time of need.

My friend, Noelia, was one of those. She was from the Dominican, had a strong personality, and was quite a bit younger than me.

David and I had spent many winters in the Dominican while he managed a winter ball team. They play winter ball in the off-season of the Major League season. Many Dominican players who spend the summer playing in the States return home to play for their "home" team.

When I met Noelia, she knew my husband managed teams in her home country. Hands on her hips, a smile on her face, but a challenge in her tone—her first question was, "Do you like my country?"

I immediately responded with, "I love your country. I like to think of it as my country too." We were so different in many

ways, but our friendship grew with the connection of "home."
The more we spent time together, the more we discovered our
commonalities.

Noelia was brilliant but never made anyone feel less intelligent, loving her family and friends deeply. She connected with women of all races and ethnicities.

Serving.

Loving.

Valuing.

Her life was cut short when she died during surgery for a broken ankle. All of her friends and family dearly miss her.

Forever Family

The deep connection of the *Forever Family* is displayed in the batterymates––pitcher and catcher. Their selfless behavior is shown in the respect and trust between the two. Their plan is implemented, with the understanding that they are working together for the best outcome of their goal to win.

The *Forever Family* is the epitome of selflessness, and they, in turn, emulate the quality. The connection makes showing humility to our friends easy because they are reliable and open to mutual love.

However, when one of the connections is prideful and self-focused, it causes the deepest pain. When the relationship is healthy, the lines blur when we emulate the selflessness quality. We pour out love naturally, never giving it a second thought.

My *Forever Family* has been my baseball family for a long time, with some additions along the way. I love the care and concern they give me and I return to them. They are a tiny group, but I leave my heart open for whomever the Lord may introduce me to that grows into my family.

Often people say professional athletes don't always show selflessness—but arrogance and vain conceit. They are humans who fall short of many people's expectations. Aren't we all victims of a failure to live up to the standard we should?

Optimistic Mindset

Not everyone will like us, and we won't like everyone, but that doesn't release us from the command to love one another. Selflessness will allow better communication with people we are in contact with at times. In our humility, we may begin to see something we like about them.

Practice showing love to everyone we come in contact with during the day. Both online and in-person contact allows us to put our wants and desires aside and respond with selflessness.

Keeping an optimistic mindset like Christ helps us think the best of others. Be excited when you see someone. Be enthusiastic about what they are doing or where they are going.

When we learn to be empathetic listeners, we strive to understand before being understood. When we listen, we immerse ourselves fully in the other person and what they are experiencing.

As we listen—not as a technique but from our hearts without agendas—we give before we receive when developing a loving relationship. Our intent listening allows the other person to open up and share.

Reflect daily on what worked and where we need more work. Commit to growing in selfless acts.

Think about the conversations we have with others. What was the focus? Were the questions asked about things that matter? Are we empathetic listeners?

Lead with a smile. Show the love of Jesus to others as we live every day. Look for opportunities to serve without expectations. Opening our ears, eyes, and spirits to where the Lord wants us to understand others' lives gives humble examples of lacking selfish ambition.

Be selfless, valuing them above ourselves.

★ ★ ★

STARTING NINE CORE QUALITY #2

Inclusion

I've never been a person who wants to be in the in-crowd. I want to include everyone in one big group of fun and encouragement.

Inclusion means the practice of providing equal access to opportunities for people who may be excluded. Inclusive love is going above and beyond to build connections with people we may never choose.

A fellow baseball wife described me as one who always looks for the left out and goes and gets them. I liked that compliment. I never want to leave someone out of connecting and being kind and considerate.

My personality draws me to those who feel like they are on the outside. I never want anyone to feel excluded. I never felt so separated until a language barrier challenged me, and I suddenly became the very thing I tried to prevent—being an outsider.

When we were in Venezuela for our first winter ball

experience, I encountered the obstacle of a language barrier. After three winters, I felt comfortable-ish with the language. Three years later, we returned to winter ball a second time in the Dominican Republic.

I didn't think Spanish would be so drastically different between the two countries. The first few times I tried to communicate in Spanish, I became very self-conscious about speaking because I couldn't understand the response. I communicated by pointing when ordering or shopping.

In Venezuela, most of the wives I encountered spoke English, which made me lazy in making an effort to speak Spanish other than in public. Many people I connected with in the Dominican spoke only Spanish, but not the one I had learned.

I began to compare myself to the group of women around me. I berated myself for not understanding or speaking the dialect of Spanish needed to communicate. I felt embarrassed and didn't want to take a risk to overcome the challenge.

Barriers Falling

Comparison is a battery of lies that change the path God has planned for us. I was allowing the enemy to use my lack of understanding of the Dominican language to hold me back. The lies I told myself grew.

I didn't want to stay in the Dominican for the winter. My hesitation to be there caused tension with my husband. I felt left out.

A few years later, David was offered another managing position in the Dominican Winter League. I prayed about the entire situation and felt the Lord challenging me to leave my unwillingness behind and spend the winter there.

I packed up the three boys in early October and moved for four months. To say I was full of fear was an understatement. I was terrified but took the first step, begging God to make it better than I expected.

Our apartment was near many stores and restaurants. We homeschooled the boys, and they went to Spanish class three times a week. I began to meet some Dominican wives who took a risk to communicate with me. Their kindness in including me in groups poured love into my heart.

The barriers fell as their love for me increased. Genuine kindness and inclusion overcame our differences, and I spent more time with the Dominican wives, players, and front office staff.

In November, we hosted a Thanksgiving dinner for all the players and staff. Typical American side dishes covered the table, along with homemade rolls. The made-from-scratch apple pie made me more lifetime friends.

A couple of months later, after their Spanish class, I joined the boys at the stadium. They went to the clubhouse, where the players and coaches hang out when not on the field. I spent time with the front office staff.

In the stadium parking lot, a group of young Dominican boys played Vitilla. Vitilla is a game played with a broomstick and a bottle cap. Some use the bottle cap from a soda bottle and others from a plastic bottle. The rules are similar to baseball, with some aspects of cricket.

Our two older boys wanted to play but were reluctant because they didn't know the kids. My husband and I encouraged them to go. They finally got up enough courage and strolled toward the group. Soon after, I saw them walking back from the parking lot, heads hung.

After a few stomps of the feet and complaining simultaneously, I realized the Dominican boys didn't want to play with my sons. One of David's Dominican native players overheard the conversation.

He asked the boys a few questions. By this time, we had forged such love for the country and people that the players knew our hearts and embraced our family.

He told my sons, "You speak like Dominicans now, but you have nice uniforms. They don't want to include you. All show, no go." He explained that the poor kids believed that when a kid had a nice uniform, they didn't know how to play.

The player gave our boys a new baseball and told my oldest to hide the ball in his back pocket, walk to the group again, and ask if they could play. He said if the boys in the group said no, pull the ball out and tell them, "Okay then, we'll just go play with the ball somewhere else."

The Dominican boys did what the player explained they would do when they saw the shiny new ball. They smiled, grabbed the boys, and included them in their game. They used a new baseball to hit with the broomstick instead of a bottle cap.

After their game, our boys told the group to keep the baseball. The Dominican boys cherished that ball. After that fun day, the group came to the clubhouse every afternoon to ask if our boys were there, baseball in hand. They played many games in that parking lot with a broomstick, a bottle cap, and a baseball.

Intentional Awareness

Being the person on the outside is a position no one wants, even if we are introverts and don't want to be around people. When left outside the perimeter of a group, we drown in loneliness.

In baseball, we have a diverse group of players and wives. They are from vastly different backgrounds and countries, speak different languages, and have different skin tones.

The makeup of baseball teams has changed over the years. Currently, the cultural dynamics are approximately 62% White, 29% Latin American/Hispanic, 7% African American, 2% Asian, and 0.4% Native American/Hawaiian/Alaska Native/Pacific Islanders. And these stats change yearly.

In the family section, where the wives and family sit during games, we see representation close to this statistic.

I've experienced that most teams have a cultural divide—this fear of being unable to communicate or misunderstanding another's culture keeps them from connecting.

The division is not always hurtful, bigoted, or prejudiced, but unfortunately, I've seen that evil too. When there is extreme division, the relationships are not as committed to long-term connections.

The teams I've been with that have the least split are the groups with whom I have the deepest bonds during the off-season or long after we aren't on the same team.

When we feel left out, we think we are the only ones. A deceptive thought, however accurate. Others feel the same and may even retreat more than us.

Keep an eye out for those sweet souls and pull them in. Intentional awareness creates a conduit for fostering relationships. When we include others, we connect by the love Christ has given us.

As we move forward, learning how to include others, we see the relationships cultivated along the way. Breaking down the barriers of comparison, we take the opportunity to love our *Accidental Acquaintances*. As we live with intentional awareness, our *Social Circles* can grow into *Kindred Spirits*. *Forever Family* creates the most accepting opportunity of including each other in love.

Honor Others

"Be devoted to one another in love.
Honor one another above yourselves."

Romans 12:10

Being devoted to and honoring others sounds like a tall order, but if we've learned to value others above ourselves, we can be devoted and honor one another.

What does devotion to one another look like in our lives? Commitment to those on the outside. Not by pretending to care but by genuinely including everyone.

Most of us have learned how to pretend to love others. We speak kindly, avoid hurting others' feelings, and fake taking an interest in them.

We may even be skilled in false care when we hear of a person's needs or become indignant when there's injustice. When we allow the Lord to break our hearts for the things that break His, we care as He does.

Jesus was an exemplary model of devotion. First, His dedication to God. He withdrew into the wilderness, on a mountain, and into a garden to pray. He purposefully spent time with God to draw closer and listen. Jesus lived His life to represent God on earth and in death for us.

He is the perfect example of kindness and love. In His earthly ministry, He blessed and served the sick, the poor, and the distraught. Jesus included the people outside, not just those closest to Him. Never was there a time of false compassion.

Eleven of the twelve disciples were loyal to Jesus. Peter denied Him three times but repented. Only one turned against Him in the end.

After Jesus' death and resurrection, Peter preached boldly and performed many miracles. Peter's actions demonstrated the source and effect of Christian power.

Because of the Holy Spirit, devoted followers were empowered so they could accomplish their tasks. The Holy Spirit is available to empower us to give us strength, courage, and insight.

God is totally committed to us. Are we dedicated to Him? Jesus is first in our lives as believers, or at least He should be. In our devotion to Him, we commit to including all of God's children.

Lifting Others

Honor means to demonstrate high respect or great esteem for someone. When we honor others, we show that we value them. We can honor for one of two reasons—either for ulterior motives or because all people are in the image of God.

Honoring people because they are created in God's image means *all* people. We are equally cared for and pay as much attention to each of our unique selves. No matter our differences, we are called to love.

Naturally, we want our beliefs to influence the people around us. God has called us to honor others even if we disagree. We are told in scripture to honor our parents, spouses, officials, and government leaders. He doesn't put an exemption policy on His command.

Lifting others doesn't mean we are lower than them or lacking in worth. We are children of a mighty God, and we can allow others to stand on our shoulders out of His overpouring of love for us.

Paul explains what it means to genuinely love others in this section of chapter twelve in Romans. He tells us not to think of ourselves more highly than we should.

We are living sacrifices, living to lay aside our desires to follow Him daily. He wants us to be transformed people with renewed minds. God has not called us to be like everyone else in the world—but has called us to ask what Jesus wants us to do.

No Favoritism

In this section of Romans 12, the title is "Love in Action." Paul gives us a guide on how to live out our faith. It begins with love and must be sincere. Sincere love is real love in the scriptural sense—loving our neighbors as we love ourselves.

Who are our neighbors? Those made in the image of God. We are called to be devoted to and honor them above ourselves.

God does not favor one over another. He may be disappointed in us, but He cares for us all. We don't get to pick and choose whom we honor. All people must be included—believers, nonbelievers, sinners, and those forgiven.

Public opinion often gets in the way of our connections. Frequently we treat people with favoritism. The well-dressed, impressive-looking person is treated better than someone who looks ragged. We do this because we incorrectly identify with success rather than failure.

Judgment according to these standards is deceptive. Because someone is distinguished-looking, we determine they are intelligent, wise, and work hard. The deception can be that they are actually greedy, dishonest, and selfish.

When we honor someone because of their appearance, we make their appearance more important than their character. If we say Christ is our Lord, we must live as He requires, showing no favoritism and loving all people regardless.

I agree that favoring like-minded people is easier than with those who disagree with our beliefs. God calls us to love our brothers and sisters in Christ. But He also tells us to go to all the nations to preach the gospel.

In Luke 6, Luke writes that we are no different from sinners if we love only those who love us or do good for only those who do good for us. We are told to love and do good to our enemies, which is extremely hard. We can do this through the help of the Holy Spirit.

Throughout Jesus' earthly ministry, He allowed the Pharisees and teachers to be near when He was teaching and healing. He let everyone benefit, while creating boundaries.

Jesus healed the exiled, bleeding woman, in a crowd that included Pharisees. The woman knew in drawing near to Jesus, with one touch of His cloak, she was healed. Jesus drew in the woman on the outside.

The Samaritan woman was ostracized from her village. Jesus

drank the water she gave Him at the well. Her past didn't deter Jesus. Public opinion didn't stop Him from showing her love.

He asked the Lord to forgive the men preparing to crucify Him. The very people who wanted to take His life, and He showed so much love by asking for their forgiveness.

We are all made in the image of God. When we accept Jesus as our Lord and Savior, we are included in the family of God. Sons and daughters of the King. At some point, when we were the one who should've been exiled or ostracized or was making bad decisions, someone included us. They loved us as we were and shared their story about their relationship with Jesus.

In the confidence of who God is and what He can do in and through our lives, an *Accidental Acquaintance, Social Circle, Kindred Spirit,* or *Forever Family* invited you into the story of God's love.

Let's be that person for someone else. Be devoted to loving those you encounter accidentally, interact with in a *Social Circle,* have a deeper connection with, and love deeply—lifting them all up.

Conduit of Connection

Many people sit for decades waiting for others to connect with them. I want to challenge you to be that conduit of connection, a channel of love to other people, even if they don't appear to want to connect. Sometimes, people need us to make the first move.

As we live out the story of God in our lives, we actively make connections. Including them in your God story requires action.

I know many of you are freaking out right now. You may

be the person who doesn't want to make a connection. Take a breath. I will not make you publicly profess your faith or your fears. Some challenges may take introverts out of their comfort zone, but I promise it's worth it in the end.

An Invitation

The year David and I returned to the Dominican with the boys for winter ball, I was purposefully growing in my faith. Earlier that year, I was unhappy and needed to put some joy back into my life. I was tentative about the whole Christian life thing, but I thought, why not give it a try?

A front office wife I had known for a few years—but never past greetings (and *saludos*) in passing—began spending time with me at the stadium during games. After a few weeks, she shared that she attended a nearby church.

She explained that it was all in Spanish but asked if I wanted to go. I jumped at the chance. I hadn't understood the Bible when I read it in English, so I thought I might try a Spanish church service.

My friend and I had attended some interesting parties in previous years, so there was no indication that we were interested in church.

Her new faith created a boldness in her, and she took a chance to invite me. Because of her kindness, I took a risk and attended her church.

Entering the service, my friend introduced me to the pastor, who immediately hugged me and told me how much the Lord loved me. My friend apologized that there wasn't an English translation. I didn't need it. God's love was being translated into my heart. She connected me to others, to her church, and to God.

Let's start with including others. Open up and let them into your moment, day, and life. We connect and build life stories together in a moment or a lifetime.

Each day, be intentional about connecting with the people you come in contact with. We never know when that one person God has placed in front of us felt left out, undervalued, and unworthy. Be the person who will help them overcome those feelings. A genuine reaction of kindness and love could be the prescription for their prayer or ours.

Accidental Acquaintance

Accidental Acquaintances may be the most challenging yet most simple when including them. They are on the outside, connecting only in passing.

The baseball examples of the first and third basemen remind me of the people on the outside. They are on opposite corners of the infield and not in contact with many players. They are more involved in more plays together than with others.

They don't get as much attention for their defense but help make plays when runners attempt to advance to their base. They motivate other teammates by generating excitement for the other players when outs are made, like a strikeout, fly ball, or double play.

Being a conduit of connection with the *Accidental Acquaintance* begins with initiating a conversation, introducing yourself, or asking a question. Sometimes it's just a smile or a quick hello.

Our efforts to include is a visible action of our devotion to God. Honoring those we have no connection to above ourselves is an example that inspires others.

Connecting with this type of relationship doesn't mean we're opening the door to our entire lives. It's a level of kindness that others they may encounter don't offer.

Holding the door for a mom entering the mall. Picking up the papers that a patron drops while standing in line at the coffee shop. Moving over a few seats at church so the elderly couple can have the end seats.

When someone pays for the coffee of the person behind them in the drive-thru, setting off a ripple of others following suit.

A stranger calls a school and pays off the accounts of students behind in their lunch payments. The parents hear of the deed and tell others, and many more schools benefit from the act of kindness.

I travel a lot during baseball seasons and with my speaking engagements. Flights and rideshares are great places to connect with *Accidental Acquaintances*.

I gauge the openness of someone sitting next to me at the airport gate, on the plane, or as the car's driver by asking a question. Like selflessness, I ask questions that initiate a thoughtful response to include the person.

I ask where they are from originally. I listen and then follow with a question relevant to their answer. Then I ask about their families. How old are their kids? What do their children want to be when they grow up? Their dream college is a good initiator of conversation.

For many, this is an easy step. For others, it may take some work. Begin to look for people in passing whom you can offer a helping hand to or someone nearby to initiate a conversation.

Social Circle

Outfielders represent the *Social Circle* regarding inclusion by needing to work together more than the corner infielders. They are essentially assigned an area to cover but sprint to help back up another outfielder or the infielders.

They combine efforts to protect the outfield. Even though each outfielder wants to protect their area solely, an outfielder will attempt with every effort to keep a ball in play and not allow it to go over the fence, robbing a home run. They combine efforts to prevent balls from dropping or passing by another player.

Honoring people within our *Social Circle* may be the easiest, but being devoted to them is where we may need to catch up. Pretending to care or be concerned comes naturally at times. We can smile and hide behind our need to move on.

Being a connection conduit, we can overcome the pretense by including them in more time together. Introduce them to other people we know. Invite them into our homes for coffee after a Bible study.

Ask them to join your softball team or play tennis or pickleball. The deeper connection with this relationship type is the invitation to linger, not just connect and retreat.

Over the years, I've moaned about never being invited to lunch or coffee. Yes, groups have asked, but I complain about the ones that don't. I became the one who invited others, and that changed the connections with many.

Our personalities may be the ones who are waiting to be invited and included, but I want to encourage you to be bold. There's no need to invite an entire room of mothers for coffee after drop-off. But we can invite one. A task met by standing firm in the knowledge that God places these people in front of us for some purpose. Don't miss out on the adventure.

Kindred Spirit

Kindred Spirits evolve out of the people you meet in your *Social Circle* when you invite them, and you realize you have such a deeper connection than before.

The *Kindred Spirits* of baseball, middle infielders, are included in most plays during a game. They are synced with each other in plays at second base. They intentionally work at being linked with every play of the game.

Some middle infielders work better together than others— their connection is cohesive and smoothly continuous. They are engaged and intentional with their fluid actions together as a double-play duo.

Taking the opportunity to instigate connections when we

intentionally see the reciprocity of interest, we own the responsibility of being conduits. We include each other in a shared belief in a more profound relationship than our *Social Circle*.

Our *Kindred Spirits* are invited into the details of our lives. We are devoted to their best interests. We ask them in with kindness and understanding, building them up in the areas where they are struggling.

Honoring them in ways that let others know we have their backs. An ebb and flow dance of one needing more than another happens throughout our time together. But it's not a problem but an honor to experience life with them.

Connecting with our *Kindred Spirits* is a natural growth of common interest. Intentional growth in conversations about what matters and what is meaningful is part of the growth. Including them in significant events is intentional.

Most of these relationships have no formal invitation but an unspoken knowing that doors are open. When the house is a mess and kids are screaming, we move to help, not sitting back and ignoring or packing up and leaving.

When I encounter someone, I want to get to know more. I love to include them in the private parts of my life. The girls I grow with to the level of *Kindred Spirit* get the more vulnerable side of me. We tell stories of hurt and pain without the fear of judgment.

These ladies know my heart, and I know theirs. I love to cheer them on without any pretense. Genuine heartfelt inclusion happens. With my baseball girls, there is no age limit and no ethnic culture or country of origin regulation.

I have developed loving relationships that have so naturally become *Kindred Spirits* that there's no answer as to how. The only reason our friendship has grown is that we connected with one another's spirits.

I am incredibly blessed that a few of these girls have stayed in my life for many years.

Forever Family

Our *Forever Family* is already included in our lives. We are connected at the hip, so they are always invited to all the fun and not-so-fun fun.

This relationship in baseball is between the batterymates, the pitcher and the catcher. They can't do what they do without each other. Starting pitchers only pitch once every five days. The catcher catches more than one pitcher during the week of games. Before every game, they intentionally produce the best plan to create the best strategy. The relationship between pitcher and catcher is stronger than any other on the field.

The *Forever Family* is so enmeshed that they purposefully plan to include each other. We are both the connectors. Invitations don't have to be formally extended because they are engaged almost daily.

Some *Forever Family* don't stay in touch each day or see each other for a while. When they connect, they engage like they've seen each other yesterday. They don't miss a beat. No need to fill in all the blanks, remembering each other's stories.

The loyalty of the relationships is based on devotion to the friendship. They are loyal beyond reason. The strong emotion of loving one another is the foundation of connection.

We honor one another by protecting each other's stories that only we know. We share more with this person than we do with anyone else. They know intimate parts of our lives.

Connection with the *Forever Family* is steeped in deep respect and great appreciation. Both reciprocate these thoughts.

They are there when we need a hug. Even if in a text or on the phone, virtual hugs can be just what we need—apps that allow us to talk with one another when not nearby.

Showing up when we have that gut feeling something is wrong. An invitation for a golf outing to talk while playing. Sitting on the beach while the family is nearby but not close enough to hear. A night out. A weekend away.

Overcoming Distance

While writing about the talking app, my Marco Polo alerted me that my friend was talking. She asked about an upcoming event in my family. I've been anxiously waiting to hear good news from my oldest son. Jenn knew I was anxious and was asking if I'd heard and if it was affecting my writing.

I included her in my feelings. She confirmed them and then said she was praying with me. The confirmation that my feelings were real helped me focus on today's task. Knowing she cared meant the world. She knows me so well.

Jenn and I live over seven hundred miles away from each other, but the miles don't matter as *Forever Family*. We overcome the distance in miles by connecting our hearts. It's in the "with."

Including one another is essential at every level of friendship. Being a conduit of connection is our responsibility at every phase.

Helping others along the way by staying aware of how they can be elevated spiritually. Continuing to be impartial and fair with whom we include allows us to continue to break down the barriers that hold us apart. Seeing what God sees in them.

Devotion and honor of one another present the love of Christ. Keep an eye out for those on the outside. Invite them to join. Initiate the conversation. Engage with intent to understand who they are. And enjoy the insanity of deep-connection inclusion.

★ ★ ★

STARTING NINE CORE QUALITY #3

Supportive

Baseball wives and girlfriends are extremely independent women. Our husbands work almost daily from February until November if they make it to the World Series.

We are in charge of everything from housing, to travel, to finances, to overseeing most family decisions. We feel like we need to make decisions on our own without anyone's help.

Sometimes it can be easy to forge ahead without support, but it can leave us lonely. We cannot do life alone. We need others. Our goal in being supportive is to be there when others need a hello, a helping hand, or a hug.

Being supportive is bearing the weight for someone with encouragement and inspiration. Supportive love is not being a stumbling block by helping others along the way with God's word and prayer.

Some of my most significant support is from my baseball family by being available for one another, communicating honestly and lovingly, praying for one another, and celebrating our lives together.

Trusted Information

After a home game, I walked toward the clubhouse and saw a usually joyous wife pale and pacing. I approached, and she immediately fell into my arms, sobbing. I hugged her until she was ready to talk.

Her husband dropped a fly ball to lose the game. To top it off, he hadn't gotten a hit to help the offense score runs during the game. Sometimes wives have meltdowns when they know their husbands will be disappointed in their play.

Wives share their despair with their closest friends so when their husbands come out of the clubhouse, they can support them without emotions making them feel bad.

Once the wife got herself together, she handed me her phone and pointed to a direct message she had received on social media. I was shocked by the offensive words written by a fan of our team.

They threatened to assault her and murder her children because of her husband's bad game. The online bully had pictures of her kids at the ballpark in the family section.

I validated her feelings of terror and told her we were there for anything she needed. I wanted her to know she was seen and had my support and prayers.

Her husband approached and wrapped his wife in a huge hug. Security took her phone. Then they went into a room to begin the investigation of the sender of the message.

All I could do at that moment was pray. This woman trusted me with the information, and I trusted God to handle the situation.

We pray that someone will be with us when something scary happens, and we need to be there when someone needs our support.

After a different game, a group of baseball ladies walked downstairs to wait for our players after an intense baseball game. We were discussing the brutal treatment of fans who sat around us. Our fellow wife's incident was fresh in our minds.

Being at our home field, we expect fans to cheer for the team. The game wasn't one of our best performances, and we lost by a lot.

The people who sat near the family section knew who the wives were, and some fans yelled insults about the women's husbands when they didn't do well. The fans booed louder and ruder at this particular game than I'd ever heard.

All the wives agreed that the fans should be cheering for the team. A security guard heard our complaints about the boos. He reminded us that if we were going to accept the claps, we had to accept the boos—a shocking response, but an honest one.

Connecting and Correcting

Supporting others includes encouraging and correcting wrong behavior. Each relationship type is different in how we do that. We learn how to discern the way we stand firm with each.

Support in sports is usually connected to the fans and their enthusiasm, or lack thereof, for their favorite team. As wives and girlfriends, we are the girders for each other to stay grounded and sustained.

The support of fellow baseball wives and girlfriends is invaluable throughout the baseball season and beyond. But sometimes there is no support at all. The culprit is usually comparison and judgment.

When we compare ourselves to others, we are almost always found lacking in our minds. It keeps us from supporting others because we can never size up to them or vice versa.

When we compare, we inevitably judge. Expressing a wrong opinion of someone is usually based on a lousy assessment of our ideas about them.

The best way to overcome comparison and judgment is to focus on others and how we can support them, rather than concentrating on our differences. Look for the people you can come alongside and where you can find that benefit for yourself.

Baseball Ministries

David and I have found incredible care from two ministries that serve in baseball—Baseball Chapel and Pro Athletes Outreach.

Baseball Chapel is an international ministry recognized by Major and Minor League Baseball and is responsible for appointing and overseeing all team chapel leaders (over five hundred throughout professional baseball).

The ministry extends throughout Major and Minor League Baseball and reaches outside the United States, serving leagues in Mexico, Puerto Rico, Venezuela, the Dominican Republic, Nicaragua, and Japan.

They also provide Sunday services and Bible studies for the home and visiting teams. They provide a women's ministry leader who runs Bible studies for the wives and girlfriends. The leaders help in many areas of life, like finding doctors, childcare, and churches.

The women's chaplain leader is also a shoulder to cry on or take along on a fun day. They are our rock in a new city with a new team.

Since 1971, Pro Athletes Outreach (PAO) has existed to unite a community of pro athletes and couples to grow as disciples of Jesus and positively impact their spheres of influence.

They seek to point the pro athlete community to pursue a life that looks more like Jesus. PAO focuses on fostering discipleship through yearly conferences, seasonal Bible studies, women's gatherings, and local events.

David and I began attending the PAO conference in 2004. It has been a place to gather with like-minded people in the baseball world. It has undergirded our relationship to withstand the time apart during the baseball season. The teachings at the conference reinforce our faith and how to serve Jesus better. We celebrate highs and pray through the lows.

We have created a support system with these connections. Our system includes informational relationships that support us with reassurance. The emotional connection shares inspiration, while the instrumental makes things work out to help. Our investigative connections snoop out where they can support us even without asking.

Make a list of ways we can support each of our relationships. We can grow in our connections and build community as we have sacred intentions, glorifying God with our *Accidental Acquaintances, Social Circles, Kindred Spirits*, and *Forever Family*.

Support is seen as one of the most important functions in relationships. When we receive support, we experience stronger coping skills and contentment. Giving support to others fills us with joy and them with peace.

By His Means

*"Therefore let us not pass judgment
on one another any longer,
but rather decide never to put a
stumbling block or hindrance
in the way of a brother."*

Romans 14:13

Ultimately each of us is accountable to Christ. Not just to each other. As believers, we must stay firm against compromising activities forbidden in scripture.

Basing our moral judgments on opinions, personal dislikes, or cultural bias rather than the word does not represent a loving Christian.

Both strong and weak Christians can cause others to stumble. Strong Christians can be insensitive and flaunt their freedom, intentionally offending others. Weak Christians may try to box others in with trivial judgment.

Paul wants readers to be strong in faith and sensitive to others' needs. We are all strong in some areas and weak in others. We must monitor the effects of our behavior on others.

We are not to be stumbling blocks to others. Taking time to support one another, we are the pillars of faith from the foundation of Christ. Be the rock of Christ where they receive the assistance needed to feel loved and supported.

Most people do not provide support because they've previously felt alone in difficult situations. I know, for me, it is challenging when I need someone to stand beside me—hold me up—and no one's there.

I have to rely on God's firm foundation during those times. Out of His tremendous love, I can feel weak in myself, but filled by Him. We cannot allow these feelings to stop us from being there for others.

Blocks placed in front of the people we meet and ourselves are frequently based on comparison. We are prideful when we compare ourselves with others or our high standards.

Comparing our strong faith to others' weaknesses is based on pride. Passing judgment causes pain to others and comes in different forms, but it should never be. Loving relationships are about seeing our differences but extending a safe place to be supported.

Comparison does not produce wisdom. As we mature in our faith, we grow in wisdom by understanding who God has created us to be. Supporting one another is a product of wisdom. Putting on love as a product of our mature faith helps us support others.

Close Connections

Elijah and Elisha were closely connected, the older mentoring the younger. They were both mighty prophets of God. Elijah was a mouthpiece for God, chosen to speak truth to the nation of Israel. Elijah had been guiding Elisha to be a strong man of God, anointing him to be his successor. Elijah neared the end of his earthly ministry. When Elijah was called to Bethel, he asked the younger man to stay where he was.

Elisha said, *"As surely as the Lord lives and as you live, I will not leave you."* They continued together to Bethel.

When they crossed the Jordan, the older man asked the younger what he could do for him before he was taken. Elisha asked to be his heir, or successor, the one to carry on the work. Elijah wasn't able to grant this request but said it was up to the Lord.

Later, a chariot of fire and horses of fire appeared and separated the two of them. Elijah went up to heaven in a whirlwind. Elisha tore his garments. He picked up Elijah's cloak, symbolizing his authority as a prophet.

The Lord granted Elisha's request because his motives were pure. His main goal was not to better or more powerful than his mentor but to accomplish more for God. Elijah and Elisha showed support to one another until the end.

The unconditional love of the Lord is what allows us to help one another. Without any obstacles in our way, we can connect and support. We can go above and beyond, stepping out of our comfort zone and releasing the potential of God's mighty power.

Above and Beyond

When Jesus entered Capernaum, someone offered their home for Jesus to preach the word. So many people gathered that there was no room left to enter. They were packed in and spilling out the door.

Four men carried a paralyzed man on a mat. They heard of the healing power of Jesus and wanted the man to benefit. Every traditional way to access Jesus was barred. So the friends, in desperation and rock-solid belief that Jesus could heal, broke through the roof and lowered the man lying on a mat in front of Jesus.

They went above and beyond for the paralyzed man because they believed in the healing power of Jesus. Jesus healed him because of his friends' faith.

Our greatest support comes from God. When we slip, His unfailing love is our foundation. We don't want to slip and hinder someone from missing the love of Christ. However, if we do make a mistake, Jesus is still there.

Jesus is the root of where we gain energy. In this strength, we can be the reinforcement someone needs.

With His help, we can be the cornerstone for relationships. Because of His power, we can be a place where people know we are committed to holding them up.

Supporting one another is sharing in our troubles. Being there to be the ear to hear, share words to encourage, pray for them and celebrate how they persevere. Care enough to strengthen others.

In Philippians 4, we read about Paul's gratitude toward the people of Philippi. He was in need, and the community supported him. He rejoiced in the concern the people showed toward him.

Paul told them he wasn't grateful just because he was desperate but because they cared enough to show their care to strengthen him. He shared that he knew how to be content in every situation, whether well-fed or hungry, in plenty or in want.

The only way he could do this was through God's strength. Then he states, *"Yet it was good of you to share in my troubles."*

Like the men who carried the paralyzed man on a mat. They shared in his troubles and found a way to help.

In our four relationships, God desires us to include all. Taking away the obstacles of judgment helps our *Accidental Acquaintance* connections. The *Social Circle* includes many, but by God's strength, we allow the group to take time to listen and become closer by serving them.

Kindred Spirits tend to embrace the close connection, allowing advice and information to be shared freely. *Forever Family* goes above and beyond togetherness, helping each other with all growth.

Setting aside our independent nature and being there to be the ear to hear, sharing encouraging words, praying for them, and celebrating how they persevere is caring enough to strengthen others.

Support Systems

Many women believe the lie that the lack or bounty of another woman determines the value of their lives. Men tend to compare their physical strength, bank accounts, and careers. Popularity is one both groups of people can relate to.

Protecting our minds from comparison, false conclusions, and assumptions is the foundation of building a supportive relationship.

Once, at a writer's conference, the speaker talked about how new writers think they will never publish because there are only so many spots for publishing. She equated it to a pie. A normal pie has six to eight pieces. It cannot be increased in size.

However, if God has called you to something, He will increase the size of that pie for us to fulfill His call. Kill comparison with that pie. Begin to support others.

When we work as team members building loving relationships rather than as isolated beings, we make a strong foundation of friends and family. Committing to taking a chance and genuinely letting others come close by offering to help build community.

Celebrating Together

Our oldest son, DJ, played baseball in college at East Carolina University during undergrad and University of Massachusetts Amherst while in grad school. He was eligible for the Major League Baseball draft after graduation.

David was coaching with the Pittsburgh Pirates that year. The day we thought DJ would be drafted, the Pirates played in Pittsburgh. He left the apartment with a silly t-shirt, and I made him change it.

He joked that if he didn't get drafted, it was because I made him change his shirt. On the chance he didn't get the call, we didn't discuss it in the family section. I didn't want him embarrassed if it didn't happen.

About the fifth inning of the nine-inning game, DJ's phone rang. A scout called and said the Washington Nationals had drafted him. When he was off the phone, he confirmed he was drafted, and I squealed so loud the wives thought something was wrong.

When I told them the Nationals drafted DJ, the celebration began. Each wife in that section stood up and cheered and hugged his neck. These ladies are forever written on my heart for their support for my son and family.

As we look for the good in others rather than seeing the bad or what we can compare ourselves to, we begin to embrace how we can be there for one another.

Leading with Grace

I've had some brutal summers in baseball and life. One of my greatest supporters over the years was a Baseball Chapel leader named Beth.

I first met Beth when I was speaking at a spring women's event for Baseball Chapel. We weren't working for the team she represented. She was there with a baseball wife who was new in her faith.

I watched them as Beth looked over the schedule of breakout sessions and asked which ones she wanted to attend. She was attentive, encouraging, and understanding.

They ended up in my class. I shared about intentional living for the Lord. At some point, I shared where I lived in the off-season. It happened to be the same city as the baseball wife.

They approached me after the session and made a connection with me. I was impressed with how Beth supported this wife without being controlling. She led this woman with grace.

I was excited when David and I discovered he'd be working with the team Beth and her husband led Baseball Chapel for. Trying not to be too weird, I observed Beth as she was empathetic but cheered on the wives in the organization. I learned so much about many things watching Beth guide women to Jesus.

Supporting others takes a loving heart. Honesty and trust are crucial. Be available when others need strength they don't have on their own.

Accidental Acquaintance

We can be a support for our *Accidental Acquaintances* in times of need. The connection is informational support.

On the baseball field, the corner infielders show support when they back up plays. Most plays rely on the individual, but they must be aware when another infielder or outfielder can't make the play and needs help.

They cover the foul territory outside the baseball field lines, exchanging verbal calls about where they are and their ability to make the play.

We realize when others struggle if we are tuned in and express empathy. Rather than passing by, stop and offer a word of encouragement or a helping hand. When we see a person struggling to carry a package, stop and help them. If a mom looks overwhelmed with wrangling the kids, offer her a smile and tell her she's got this. Empathy is key.

At the ballpark, I encounter people I don't know every day, but I can support them in some way. A smile and a gentle word can show we are there for them.

The dad in the stadium who lost a kid. The kid couldn't wait one more minute in line for food because they wanted to see the play, which caused a burst of excitement. We can point out where the kid ran and offer to stand in the father's place in line until he retrieves the kid.

Grandpa drops his wallet and can't quite reach it under his seat. We can lean down and return it with a smile. Pass the money or card to the person in the middle of the row who wants that ballpark frank. Communicating support without words works too.

We must overcome the uncomfortable feelings of stepping into a space where we shouldn't be and not let judgment or comparison stop us from helping.

Social Circle

In our *Social Circle*, more opportunities exist to provide support in an emotionally connected network.

The outfielders are involved in plays together, backing each other up, and the infielders on plays. When good plays are made, players celebrate collaboration and success.

When my kids were playing Little League Baseball, it seemed like they each needed something different at the same time. I was amazed at how the moms around me reached out to help.

The middle son needed the restroom now. The oldest needed his glove strings tied now. The youngest was starving to death and needed food now.

"How can I help you?" another mom asked. One mom grabbed the glove while another pulled out snacks because I forgot to bring any. I ran to the bathroom while the moms had my back. We helped each other a lot during those games.

Sitting in those chairs on the edge of the field opened up a chance to ask questions and explore faith in a fun, no-pressure environment.

At Bible study at my home church, a woman sitting next to me was a bit tentative being in the group. I introduced myself and asked if this was her first time. She confirmed it was, and it was her first time attending any Bible study. I listened with an empathetic heart and responded with loving guidance.

I reassured her she was welcome and shared my Bible during the teaching. She reiterated that she was embarrassed not to know as much as others. I told her that was normal and that I would pray for her as she journeyed through the study.

Be the rock for others who are struggling, not a block for them to stumble. Give a word of encouragement. Hold out your hand to lift them. Be present when in a conversation, without judgmental body language, acknowledging their concerns.

Kindred Spirit

Kindred Spirits create a deeper connection of strength for one another. The association is instrumental in bearing the weight of their needs.

The middle infielders are well-established in assisting one another without much hindrance. They read the weakness of the other and provide strength. As the double-play combo, their strength is in the assistance given and backing up plays.

This relationship is where we begin to establish our support system. We are more available because we spend more time together and understand each other's needs. Our connection gives us a safe place to be the reinforcement when others need it most. Be an instrument of support.

We prioritize time with them by making ourselves available, maybe not in person but by answering their calls or responding to a text. Our visits with them may not be quantity of time but are full of quality.

They are the group who returns the support. We can call and know they will talk. Often, we have a few in this group whom we can ask for prayer.

However, with this connection, we speak with loving guidance but also give and receive grace-filled correction. Kindness and wisdom guide us in words of grace when correcting our *Kindred Spirits* and when they correct us.

Through this guidance, our relationships created on mutual Christian faith can strengthen and hold up our connections.

When someone needs a boost, we celebrate. Gathering to shine the light on a person nourishes the love in the relationship. We gather with others but know our *Kindred Spirit* connections are special because of the built trust and vulnerability.

In baseball, these connections spend more time with us than others. Women are not ignored. Our time together is important. If we cannot connect at the ballpark during games, we gather before the game to intentionally connect. We are like a gadget that makes life easier.

Our talks are more vulnerable and transparent. We may pull each other aside to share our hearts. We understand each other's needs without verbal clues that we need some alone time.

My friend who had the death threat via a social media message called me after she got home. "I'm letting fear win. I need you to pray, and I just want to listen."

Our husbands left for a road trip after the game. Security

was on top of the threat, and the man was arrested. They promised her that she was safe. But she needed reassurance that God was with her and would protect her.

I prayed for a while. She stayed quiet. I read scripture and prayed scriptural words of comfort over her. Paralyzed by fear, she couldn't function when she first called. I carried her mat to the feet of Jesus through prayer and scripture.

We understood each other on a deeper level because of our faith. We had no judgment or comparison that kept us separated. Our love for Christ connected us.

Forever Family

Forever Family support is the next step of a support system. I consider them our investigators in the support system. They are aware of the needs most of the time, even without others sharing. If they feel something is wrong but get no confirmation, they will dig until they unearth the issue.

The pitcher and catcher are the most supportive combination on the team. A pitcher pitches the ball as best he can, and if he's the slightest bit off, the catcher frames the catch to hopefully trick the umpire into believing it was a strike.

If the pitcher is not having his best outing, the catcher will go to the mound and help him make corrections. The catcher is usually the only one to sit with him on the bench in the dugout. The support system between these two is continually inquiring about the needs of the other.

The *Forever Family* is the most important in our support system. They are like the supports that hold up a bridge. The relationship's foundation is so deep in the ground that there is very little wavering, especially when struggling.

They provide the strength needed to hold them up. They are available for late-night calls or texts. There is no delay in reading or responding. They check in regularly and visit often, even if not invited. They don't just enjoy the quality of time but also make an effort for the quantity of time.

They are present and show extreme empathy. They never talk behind the other's back. They have meaningful conversations of loving correction.

These relationships don't judge each other because they are usually too busy laughing at the silliness between them. *Forever Family* doesn't just pray when asked. They pray daily for each other.

In each of these connections, sometimes breakdowns of communication happen. We may try our hardest with *Kindred Spirits* and *Forever Family* to never breach such hurt, but we are human and fail.

I encourage you to forgive if someone hurts you. Forgive yourself and them. Please don't allow it to stop you from supporting others when they are in need.

We entrust our stories to one another, not allowing our preconceived thoughts to create stumbling blocks to growing deeper relationships. Be supportive of one another so we can inspire growth in loving relationships.

★ ★ ★

STARTING NINE CORE QUALITY #4

Peacemaker

For most of my life, I had relationships that were constantly at odds. I didn't feel safe because of all the unrest. It's challenging to be the one wanting harmony, when others want trouble.

I didn't always help with unity because I was highly defensive in these relationships and with everyone I interacted with. I had no calmness in my soul, so I couldn't share anything but chaos.

I carried that turmoil into my early adult years. Wanting to feel calm, I chased different ways to grasp it.

I worked and worked, trying to put mind over matter. *Think about peace, and you will have it,* is what I thought would happen, but it didn't.

Only when I began to trust Christ and truly embrace the inner calm He desires, beyond my understanding, did calm abound.

Jesus transformed me. I began turning my defensive attitude into being the one who emulated unity. I turned from bad intentions to expecting good. I sought God's love and pursued it in my connections.

A peacemaker is described as one who brings about peace. Peace-loving means using God's love to create loving relationships, even in chaos.

Anything but Peace

Growing up, I couldn't express opinions contrary to others around me. Hurtful words and demeaning comments would follow. Arguments would turn into physical threats, and I would be the first to be ready to brawl.

Then as an emerging adult, I was exposed to more open-minded groups of people who discussed opinions and didn't want to fist fight.

Like my friend who received death threats through a direct message, many of us find that sharing something we don't even think might lead to controversy causes an onslaught of attacks.

We must make every effort to do what leads to tranquility. But life. At every turn, someone seems to want to stir up controversy. Everyone has an opinion, and most don't care whom they hurt trying to prove themselves right.

There always seems to be a group of people that feel they can cut down others with gossip and sharp words. Reputations are ruined, friendships destroyed.

Conflict is a fight, battle, or war between people because of differing opinions, attitudes, understandings, or interests. The loss of peace and harmony is the result.

Friction and discord start in our hearts. We choose whether to instigate problems or bring unity during a conflict.

"Have you met his girlfriend yet?" The woman whispered in my ear as she pointed to a player standing outside the clubhouse.

"Yes?" I hesitantly replied with more of a question than a statement.

Her insensitive tone alerted me of unkind words to follow. I sent the boys off to play with a group of kids.

She squawked a rant immediately after the boys left, "You don't really know who she is when you meet her. She seems nice, but she's faking it. She's a real ..." Her nasty profanity hurt me. I felt so sorry for the woman she was talking about. She was leaning toward humiliation.

The player's girlfriend was so sweet. She was kind to my kids and me. Her husband was respectful of my husband. I didn't know her well. I had sat with her by the pool during spring training, and we talked again when we bumped into them at restaurants. I liked her.

I asked her why she didn't attend games. She said she had to work. She seemed hesitant when the excuse was offered, but there were no red flags. She was actually lovely.

Being on a new team had brought a new group of women, and after the tirade from one wife, these women would be a bit of work.

When women cut others' characters, it contaminates the mind of the people listening. The person they are talking about doesn't have a chance to defend themselves. They plant seeds of negative thoughts.

During the first few weeks of baseball's regular season, I try to meet all the wives and girlfriends to assess the atmosphere.

Within that time, we usually have Bible study. The women that attend typically are on their best behavior when in this group. It takes a while to flesh out the personalities and assess how to approach the groups.

The player's wife, gossiping about a different player's girlfriend, told anyone around her how awful the girlfriend was. Things said were exaggerated for the wife's benefit at the girlfriend's expense.

It broke my heart to hear the condescending words spoken.

I've received them quite a few times from people close to me and others that were not so close.

I've also been on the giving end of being a blabbermouth to try and elevate my standing with others by cutting someone in two. I thank God that He has changed my heart and helped me learn to be a peacemaker, not a glory thief.

Conflict and Opportunity

A glory thief steals all the joy and honor from people. When I began to equate the glory of Jesus to me, I turned from evil thoughts and words and tried to do good instead, giving all the glory to Him, not me.

The girlfriend under attack didn't sit in the family section once the season started. She never came into the family room. She sat in a faraway section and waited in her car after the game, which didn't give her many opportunities to connect.

I sought her out and began to know her for who she really was, not the words spoken about her. I never spoke of the wife's condemnation of her but tried to include her in group activities. She declined over and over.

The cantankerous relationship had been developing for many years. I wanted to retaliate against the wife who degraded the girlfriend, but I knew that wouldn't help. It would just be joining into evil intent.

It seemed like there was no way to defend the girl under attack. Retreating seemed like a better way to handle the situation. Fight or flight, right? The girlfriend believed she couldn't fight the wife to defend herself, so she avoided it. I was feeling the same way.

I knew that wasn't the way to handle the controversy. When idle gossip and hurtful accusations fly, the only choice we have to rectify or heal is to be the peacemaker.

Conflict is an opportunity to glorify God. As we grow to be

more like Christ, we can overcome the destruction of relationships and begin to build them in love.

Instead of retaliating, joining in, or retreating, we can purposefully help bring peace. We must strive for complete restoration by encouraging unity among each other. However, it's not always the reality and is rarely easy.

I've learned that not all relationships can continue or even be healed. We cannot control people's desire to cause issues. I've had to limit contact and say no to requests. Sometimes, the only way to get calmness is to break the connections.

Some relationships need strict boundaries or complete release. We never want to stop loving others, but we must understand what helps and what doesn't. Separating ourselves from all activities is not healthy.

I couldn't stop the wife from verbally attacking the girlfriend, but I was able to set an example of building loving relationships for the other girls.

I prayed for unity among the larger group of wives. I watched for unrest and tried to redirect conversations to the truth. I refused to join in the gossip or the degrading of anyone.

Being the reconciler wasn't always accepted by all of the women. But I persevered in the uncomfortable.

When there was a bit of turmoil, I responded in love rather than retaliate or retreat. I chose to bring calm rather than chaos.

For *Accidental Acquaintances*, we are brokers of peace, practicing restraint. *Social Circles* grow when conflict is dealt with early. *Kindred Spirits* are carriers of peace for one another. *Forever Family* cherishes one another because they cherish the peace they find within their relationship.

As we learn to be peacemakers, we will find more harmony in our lives and relationships. We can bring peace to each connection.

Prepare for the Long Journey

"They must turn from evil and do good;
they must seek peace and pursue it."

1 Peter 3:11

Peter advises us to turn from evil and do good. The church has many people who are characterized by shameful attitudes and actions—damaging relationships with God and others.

When Peter wrote *they,* he meant us. He urges us to turn from evil and to do good. We don't always think what we do is evil, but if it is not God-honoring, it is not good.

People sin. But we, as believers, need to bring calmness to every connection. Peace is produced by consciously overcoming evil and asking God to bring peace to all.

But Jesus tells us that others will know we are disciples by loving others. Peter repeats this command in verse 8, along with the need to be sympathetic and compassionate.

Peace is the translation from the Hebrew word *shalom,* a standard greeting by the Jews. The word *shalom* does not mean the absence of troubles or worries. It refers to a deep sense of wholeness, translated as wellness. *Shalom* is used to describe a personal, inward, and lasting peace.

The peace Jesus is talking about here is the inner calmness in your heart, despite troubles. It does not depend on your circumstances, nor does it remove worries or anxieties. But it gives you the ability to endure with strong confidence that God will see you through.

The biblical definition is being still and confident in times of trouble because God is with us. Being a peacemaker means using God's love to create loving relationships.

When we seek peace, we are looking for God in every

situation. We are attempting to find love with a desire to obtain it. The word seek tells us that finding it can be challenging. We investigate it continually.

Pursue is an active verb meaning to actively follow after and try to chase it down. It is a drive to continually and actively try to find peace. It may be a long journey, but we're to keep going.

Pursuing Peace

Too often, we think it is merely the absence of conflict. Many see peacemaking as a passive role. To be effective, we actively pursue harmony. A by-product of our commitment to building good relationships, the peacemaker anticipates problems and deals with them before they occur—therefore, peacemaking is a process.

Peacekeepers keep harmony by making sure things are kept in order. A peacemaker makes things happen by pursuing freedom from strife between people. They compromise themselves in the hope of keeping the peace between people.

We bring unity by not avoiding nor appeasing. We emulate tranquility in conflict and use appropriate responses to lead back to truth and the attitude of love.

We cannot be peacemakers unless we first make a connection with God. We must repent of our wrongs and turn away from them.

Trusting God and His plans for our lives, not relying on our understanding, is the groundwork.

When we are insulted or hurt, we are to be a blessing so that we will inherit a blessing. God blesses us with every spiritual gift.

Blessed means more than happiness. It implies a desirable state for those who are believers. As a Christian, blessed means an experience of hope and joy in all situations.

To access these blessings, we turn from evil and do good. We are children of God. He tells us we are not only to seek peace but also to pursue it.

Pursuing the Prince of Peace

In Isaiah, Jesus is called the Prince of Peace. He is the only reason we can truly live our life with God. Living in harmony with God's creatures is being in right relationship with Him. He restores broken relationships. With the love of God, we will see heaven on earth in our relationships.

The disciples saw Jesus face-to-face and forgot what Jesus taught. In John, Jesus promised the disciples that the Holy Spirit would help them remember what He taught them. This promise would help the disciples remember, without taking away their perspectives. We also have access to this potential.

The Holy Spirit helps us trust God to plant truth in our minds, convincing us of God's power. The Holy Spirit's work in our lives results in profound and lasting peace. It is the confident assurance that we do not need to fear any struggle. The peace of God moves into our hearts and lives to offer comfort where there is conflict.

The apostle Paul was a great peacemaker. For much of his life, he persecuted Christians. With arrest warrants, Paul traveled over 150 miles from Jerusalem to Damascus to hunt down Jewish Christians.

On that road, he was stopped by a blinding flash of light and a heavenly voice. It was Jesus. Not the dead troublemaker Saul believed Him to be, but the risen Lord. His encounter with Jesus transformed Paul. He changed Paul's life forever.

Paul humbled himself and learned not to retaliate, join in, or retreat. He confronted conflict with truth. He stood firm in his beliefs, continuing to spread the teachings of Jesus even from prison.

He became one of the most influential leaders in the early Christian church. He continues to teach through the books of the Bible. He wrote at least thirteen of the books in the New Testament.

While sitting in a Roman prison, he didn't know if he would be released or put to death. He had many reasons to be anxious, defensive, and angry. He chose peace.

Paul writes the word *peace* over fifty times in scripture. He encourages us to be spiritually minded, which brings life and peace.

He gave us excellent guidance through submitting to the Lord in every situation and with every person he encountered. He kept his focus on Jesus and the gospel.

Surrendering ourselves to God in our relationships helps us be calm, which is needed. Christ is the reason we can live in harmony. Jesus brought the good news to all people.

Jesus provides unity with God, our families, and others we are in contact with daily. We can be peacemakers when we seek and pursue the Prince of Peace.

There is no end to Jesus' eternal peace. Without God's love within ourselves, we cannot live tranquilly with others. Ask the Lord to fill you with His peace before entering any relationship.

With Jesus, all of our connections are based on the eternal peace we receive from Him. When we strive for peace each day, our *Accidental Acquaintances* see it, but they may not understand it. *Social Circles* make compromises to maintain harmony within the group. Our *Forever Family* are our safe place of tranquility, sharing Jesus' peace.

Becoming a Peacemaker

When building the nine core qualities as a foundation of loving relationships, we will find some to be easier than others. Peacemaking takes effort, but it is well worth the work.

Running from conflict is a natural response for some; others may stand up and fight until the bitter end. I want us to learn how to stand firm, turn from evil to good, seek peace in our relationships, and cultivate gentle spirits.

Peacemakers bring God's peace to relationships. Let peace rule in our hearts by stepping out as active explorers and chasers of goodwill. Continually cultivate a gentle spirit of love.

Be patient with all people and continue to forgive others and ourselves along the way. Continual growth in our connection with the Lord and forgiveness cultivates loving relationships.

The steps to being a peacemaker with all associations are to stop conflicts from arising, think of ways to bring harmony, apply boundaries, and respond in love. Cultivate a gentle spirit. Look at these steps in each of the four relationship types.

Accidental Acquaintance

In *Accidental Acquaintance* relationships, we are responsible for bringing calm, not turmoil.

In baseball, the first and third basemen primarily work independently. However, when an infield play happens, the infielders, pitchers, and catcher could have the potential to make a play.

An infield fly ball, a bunt, or a dribble hit can bring them into the action. Reading other players' movements should happen, but it does not always. The conflict arises when players don't trust the other's ability, they collide, or no one makes the play.

Finding things to discuss with an *Accidental Acquaintance* that don't cause conflict stops many people from connecting. Many topics strangers can argue about. Open up social media, and you see that ninety-nine percent of issues can cause an argument.

When beginning conversations, I use the percentage rule, finding the one percent we can agree on and ignoring the ninety-nine percent we don't.

Embracing the percentage rule of finding what you can agree on and giving it all your attention promotes peace. Leaving the ninety-nine and leaning into the one percent stops conflicts.

Seeking and pursuing peace with these connections is maintaining the ability to think of these topics that bring peace. When disagreements arise, we must apply boundaries. At this level of connection, always respond with love, but sometimes walking away can be the answer.

Another connection at this level is online associations. Our peacemaking skills need to be at the forefront with social media and other apps that put us in contact with people we may never meet or have known over time.

The internet can be toxic, yet we need to be the stabilizing. humble personalities people see. Remember, the accounts are real people who have real hurts but may be covering them up with filters.

Pray for others when you see accounts that are argumentative or even unreasonable. Show self-control in responding. How can God be glorified in the situation? If He cannot, then stay silent.

Stay away from opinions that could escalate the negativity. Correcting others is not always an excellent way to decrease attacks. Gentle replies often disarm them.

Social Circle

Our *Social Circle* necessitates more work to maintain peace. Outfielders stop conflicts from arising by working as independent entities and being the backup for plays where they are needed. When they make plays together, they work to help the other player, creating boundaries by communicating when needed.

The gathering of people within our *Social Circle* means we are in closer contact than *Accidental Acquaintances*. Pray for peace before entering a room or a relationship. Ask for peace where you meet them and within these relationships.

In any group, we can encounter people who are annoying and rub on our last nerve. In our *Social Circle*, we come in contact with them more often.

These people can push us to explode with anger or frustration. When we have prayed for peace, we can respond in love rather than rage.

If we see issues rising, we must recognize the problem and deal with the conflicts early. Because of the closer connection, all disputes should be brought into the open and dealt with before they become unmanageable.

Deep unresolved resentment usually doesn't exist in this group, but it can be the root of future irritation and problems. When we don't confront uncomfortable circumstances, bitterness can take hold.

Taking control of any self-defense and holding our tongue is a bit easier with this group because of our minimal history with them. But to create peace, we must regulate our reactions and respond peacefully.

Bring peace by paying attention to the conversation, redirecting when needed, and finding the one percent to discuss. Take only small steps into the ninety-nine percent, watching for conflicts.

We can physically bring peace. Food brings joy to many groups. I believe it should be added as a love language and a unifier. It can also be brought as a peace offering. Sharing food and recipes can cause conversations to be directed into a calmer, less testy talk.

Kindred Spirits

Kindred Spirits have a much closer connection, and peacemaking is essential for this group.

The second baseman and shortstop cannot work smoothly

together in conflict. If ego or unrealistic expectations get in the way, this affects their potential to turn double plays. They must keep harmony between them to be effective.

Our *Kindred Spirit* connections rely on bringing peace into the relationship. Both should pray for peace in the relationship, but one prays more often than the other. The one who hasn't been as much of a prayer instigator jumps into that position when needed. They take turns bringing peace.

They recognize disagreements when they first arise. In a healthy connection, they confront the problem before it escalates. When they do not, the difficulty can break apart their link. In a healthy state, they both bring peace. If one doesn't, the other picks up the balance.

The most significant difference between the *Social Circle* and *Kindred Spirits* is that the latter moves into reconciliation and avoids getting stuck in resentment when a problem arises.

Kindred Spirits bring the conflict to the table and have a heart-to-heart talk. They apply boundaries around the things that cause issues.

Forever Family

Conflict is often directed toward others, not each other, because they have each other's backs like the *Forever Family*.

The *Forever Family* takes the stance of the *Kindred Spirit*, but takes it further.

In the deep connection between the pitcher and catcher, they are too busy working for the betterment of each other and the entire team to want to create turmoil.

In our relationships, this profound connection intentionally seeks and pursues peace with their relationships.

They have each other's back in challenging situations, realizing the issues the instant they arise. Resentment is not in their hearts, so reconciliation happens early in uncomfortable circumstances.

Self-control with our *Forever Family* isn't to avoid uncomfortable topics but to ensure we aren't inadvertently hurting someone with hurtful words. The percentage rule grows skewed in these connections. We venture more into the ninety-nine percent, even if we disagree.

We pray for peace and God's goodness for each other. Usually, we can discuss more challenging topics without taking things personally and being hurt.

Being quarrelsome is never a benefit for the relationship. Arguments cause division. *Forever Family* avoids many things that cause separation.

Inner attitudes are voiced in a nonconfrontational way. We do not cause anger in the other, making sure to present issues with love. If there is something that the other is doing wrong or against their beliefs, we bring it up to help the other, not harm.

On the Team

God brought peace when Jesus died on the cross. His Holy Spirit lives within us, carrying that peace with us in every circumstance. We rely on Him to bring peace into our associations.

Jesus is looking for the star of the team of peacemakers. Someone who shows self-control in responding to turmoil. One who thinks about God's word when confronting issues and shows affection to people who aren't easy to love. He is looking for the person responsible for bringing peace into our connections with others.

Prepare for the long journey in these different contacts. When deep wounds or hurtful words remain, it will not be easy. Loving one another before receiving love in return prepares our relationships for growth.

We can make peace with others who are difficult. Many people are in such pain that they are perpetually defensive.

Our ability to be calm and nonconfrontational helps bring peace to them.

When we bring solidarity to each relationship, we can be who God desires us to be. Continue to bring shalom.

Seek and pursue peace in every circumstance. As we learn to see problems, we can avoid the things that cause the issues.

Then, we know to hold our tongues on matters that do not need to be brought up and to take a conversation in a different direction. Restrain from saying too much. There is no benefit from dumping words on another.

Create boundaries with those who cannot return the love given. Take the first step to ensure that people around you know what you will and will not discuss.

Determine what topics will be avoided and which issues are discussable. Naming those issues helps keep a caution on the things that can cause division.

When hurt happens, first take it to God. Then ask the person to meet in a neutral place to share your pain, not to blame, but to share and let them know how you felt when they acted the way they did. Be ready to reconcile.

If people need help in their relationships, we can step in to bring them together. Helping others reunite with Christ is the first step.

When forgiveness is needed in a relationship, forgive or urge someone else to do so. Forgiving those who have hurt us and asking for forgiveness of those we've hurt reconnects.

As we aim to be humble, we choose to avoid foolish arguments. Be kind to everyone, bringing integrity and love. Cherish peace where we find it and where we bring it. Peacemakers bring glory to God in our relationships, encouraging peace.

We are the initiators of bringing peace into relationships. Begin with prayer. Think about where you can physically offer calm and love. Create a team of peacemakers.

★ ★ ★

STARTING NINE CORE QUALITY #5

Encouraging

Encourage means putting courage into someone's spirit. The prefix -en root means "in" or "into" in Latin and French origins. Courage finds its beginnings in the French *corage*, meaning "heart" as the seat of emotions, spirit, temperament, or frame of mind.

Also, the Latin *cor* means heart. Merriam-Webster defines *encourage* as "to inspire with courage, spirit, or hope" and "to spur [one] on." As we encourage others, we are infusing them with courage.

We aren't to speak phony niceness but God-laced words of courage that go straight to the heart. If we are encouraging, we are actively building the bravery of another and motivating others in love and kindness. We are created as relational beings, meant to interact to uplift one another.

Discouraged people are all around us—even us sometimes. We are deprived or drained of courage or confidence. Our hearts feel empty. We wonder if we will ever find our way back to community or a life of joy.

Despair and anxiety have always been and will always be a part of our world. God wants to fill us with the Holy Spirit to guide us to provide the hope we have in Him to others. We can all find strength and bravery in Jesus.

Real community is not life-depleting but life-enriching. As we encounter people daily, I want us to learn how to affirm others, strengthening them to stand confidently.

Speaking healing truth over the wounds of others cultivates a safe environment. Be a life-giving presence. We must let down our guard and be all-in encouragers.

A Needed Boost

At a low point in my life, a fellow baseball wife showed up and helped me take the next step. She didn't even know how much pain and suffering I was experiencing.

David and I were at rock bottom in our marriage, but had committed to working on it together. I lacked the hope that we could rectify our broken connection. I was lonely and sad and didn't want anyone to know.

At the ballpark during spring training, the boys were on the field with David, and I sat on a bench outside the fence. A fellow baseball wife joined me on the metal seating.

We chatted about our off-season and how much the kids had grown. She discussed her job and how she hoped for children one day but didn't know how it would work out.

I shared how I handled being a nurse when the boys were younger and now I chose to stay at home. She understood the demands of baseball and how our husbands weren't available much during the season.

She told me about a Bible study she was leading at a local church. They scheduled it on days the guys could be with the kids before going to the ballpark. She didn't ask where I was in my faith or if I went to church. She just invited me.

I hesitated at first. I thought she would not want me there if she knew how broken I felt. But she insisted, saying she thought I would love to be around other women in baseball.

"I'll pick you up, and we can go together," she enthusiastically stated. "I'd love to get to know you better." Without a response from me, she stood. "Well, that's that. I'll see you Tuesday morning in front of the hotel."

Her invitation was the boost I needed. I wasn't brave enough to go on my own. She gave me hope. Someone wanted to get to know me and went out of their way to include me.

I've never forgotten the gesture of love and encouragement. And I have tried to emulate that ministry of encouragement. Her ability to be present with me gave me confidence and redirected my despair to hope.

Initiate a Cheer

A boisterous crowd in a baseball stadium can change the momentum of games. When the crowd gets invigorated with chants and loud outbursts, it can be the catalyst for a team to take the lead.

I was a cheerleader in high school. I was good at it because I was loud and had no qualms about getting the crowd riled up for games.

Pep rallies were my favorite. The entire school would enter the football stadium or gym. I would find the kids in the school who loved to assist in promoting rambunctious responses to our cheers.

A couple of the other girls and I would also approach the quieter kids in the stands. They weren't eager to participate in the pep rally, but when we initiated a cheer in front of them and shook our pom-poms vigorously, begging them to respond, they would begin with a slight grin and then join in.

I made many connections in high school with many who didn't feel like they fit in with the cheerleaders or athletes but became part of the team and answered the call enthusiastically.

I've led a few cheers in the stands during baseball games. The playoffs are the best place to get excited and give high fives to everyone around when great plays happen or after a win. The atmosphere is electric with excitement.

My life has been one of being a cheerleader for others. I love infusing love, hope, and joy into the lives of others and picking out one thing that shines through them. Or when someone is battling grief, being there for them and pointing them to hope.

I wasn't always as bold without pom-poms. My boldness came with my growing faith. After the baseball wife invited me to her Bible study, I became more curious about Jesus.

As my faith strengthened, so did I. The Holy Spirit filled me with courage. I became more confident in connecting with others and uplifting them. Love poured out.

Sometimes I didn't feel like boosting others because I feared their response or was ill-equipped. Focusing on God, I overcame the fear of rejection and the inability to bond.

One year, I watched a young girl sit alone and not talk with anyone. At that point, I wasn't sure if she was a sister, wife, or girlfriend.

When I finally introduced myself, she was eager to talk. I heard she and her new husband met in November and married in February before coming to spring training. She wasn't sure how to navigate the new and foreign lifestyle she encountered.

Over the years, I've offered a Bible study for the girls on whatever team we were on. I invited her to join us at a backfield picnic table. Nothing fancy, just a bunch of girls with their Bibles. She didn't have a Bible, so I offered to bring one.

I loved seeing her connect with Jesus at each of our studies. I became a cheerleader for her, and the other girls embraced her and helped her learn to navigate baseball life.

Our words of encouragement are life-giving power. However, we all know people who only share life-draining words.

Uplifting others when they are not there for you may be awkward, but it becomes more natural as we tap into God's healing power for our hearts and souls.

Encouraging people inspire others to be better than before. They uplift them emotionally, physically, and spiritually. They are bold and take a chance to help others push through. *Accidental Acquaintances* are encouraged through a smile. *Social Circles* are uplifted with kind words.

Kindred Spirits are inspired through serving one another when it's unexpected, and *Forever Family* are motivated by one another even in the quiet.

We inspire curiosity in others when we introduce courage to overcome fear, loss, or anger. With courage, confidence builds, and they are inspired and motivated to build up others in response.

Building Up

"Therefore encourage one another
and build each other up,
just as in fact you are doing."

1 Thessalonians 5:11

Paul instructs us to encourage and build each other up. He then urges us on by believing we are already encouraging others in the middle of his teaching.

He knew God doesn't just recommend encouragement. He commands it, knowing we need a boost from others.

God tells us we will have trouble in the world, but He has

overcome it. Our world is broken and can lead many to despair and discouragement. People are hurting. It isn't our job to judge whether they should be brokenhearted. We are instructed to encourage and build each other up.

Words can be giving or draining. James compares the damage the tongue can do to a raging fire. An uncontrolled tongue can cause terrible pain. A few words spoken in anger can destroy a relationship that takes years to build or inhibit a connection from initiating.

Before we speak, we remember that we cannot reverse the damage that harsh words can do but we can bring about connections with inspiring words.

The Bible gives us many scriptures to encourage one another. Instructing us not to let harmful words be spoken is only what lifts another. Gathering together helps us spur one another on in love and good deeds. And to encourage one another with God's word.

These theological truths aren't just personal knowledge but a collective education. Scripture is full of encouraging Bible verses of hope and inspiration. God wants to comfort us and inspire others in our response to His love.

Encouragement is God's healing power for our hearts as we tap into the healing and loving words of Jesus. Encouragement fosters loving relationships.

A word of encouragement offered at the right moment can make the difference between connecting with someone or not.

Love is indispensable. No matter what words we speak without love, the sound of those words is nothing more than a clanging cymbal. Loving words are used to seek the well-being of another.

First Corinthians 13 gives us nine ways to build others up. We hear this passage at most weddings, but these spiritual gifts can be used with any connection.

Love is patient and kind, does not envy or boast, and is not proud. It doesn't dishonor and is not self-seeking, not easily angered, and keeps no record of wrongs. Love doesn't delight in evil, but love rejoices in the truth. It always protects, trusts, hopes, and perseveres. Love never fails.

Love that protects, trusts, hopes, and perseveres allows us to give love to others freely. Putting our selfish intent behind us and striving to encourage and build others up permits us to show love while expecting nothing in return.

The more we love like Christ and share His word, the more our encouragement leads others to Jesus.

Biblical Encouragers

After the death of Moses, Joshua was appointed as Israel's leader. Because Joshua was Moses' assistant for many years, he was well prepared. Joshua's new job was to lead two million people into a foreign land and conquer it.

God promised Joshua that He would fulfill the promises He made to Moses. God told Joshua He would be with him. Then in the following few verses, God told him to be strong and courageous.

The promises of God are life-changing. They enable us to inspire and motivate others. We can build others up when we know that God is with us and we are to be strong and courageous.

As we focus on Jesus, we can take our eyes off ourselves and pour out to others. As we meditate on scripture, we are motivated to love others as we want to be cared for by them.

The author of Hebrews tells us to encourage one another daily. As long as it is today, we should express it with love and concern.

A man named Joseph was such an encourager that he earned the name "Son of Encouragement," or Barnabas. He was drawn to the people he could encourage. Through his helpful actions toward Christians, non-Christians were drawn to him.

After Paul's conversion on the road to Damascus, he arrived in Jerusalem. The local Christians were terrified by his presence because of his history of attacking believers.

Barnabas risked his life to meet with Paul. He could discern Paul's honesty and told others that their former enemy was now a follower of Christ.

The persecution of Christians had scattered believers, and the gospel went with them. The church sent Barnabas to investigate what was happening in Antioch. He was pleased with what he found. When he returned to Tarsus, he asked Paul to return with him.

Later, Barnabas inspired Mark to go with him and Paul to Antioch. Mark had made a few foolish mistakes along the way but just needed some time and support. He was eager to do the right thing but struggled with completing tasks.

Mark joined Paul and Barnabas on their first missionary journey. On their second stop, Mark returned to Jerusalem. Finding Mark's actions unacceptable, Paul denied Barnabas' request to have Mark travel with them again. The partners went separate ways, Paul with Silas and Barnabas with Mark.

The separation doubled the missionary effort. Barnabas was patient with Mark, investing in him as a man of God. His enduring reassurance boosted Mark's ministry.

Rarely is there a situation when there is no one to build up with the love of Christ. We often jump into criticism about assumptions we make, pointing out a person's deficiencies.

Barnabas shows us that encouragement is one of the most effective ways to help others. His obedience to God and kindness to others were quiet but impactful. He was a good man full of the Holy Spirit. His gentle inspiration drew many to the Lord.

Barnabas showed patience with Mark, and others noticed. When we are jealous of others, we cannot see the gifts they have been given and celebrate with them. We often confuse our need to encourage others with needing to be uplifted.

When we fully believe the Lord is with us and become strong and courageous, we can inspire and motivate others to be the same. Grace-laced words of scripture build up the spiritual lives of others. When we provide encouragement in tangible ways, it lifts the hearts of our connections.

Actively look for people who need to be infused with courage. The *Accidental Acquaintance* who looks like they're struggling. Share a compliment, being specific. In our *Social Circle*, is there someone who needs prayer? Pray on the spot. Send letters of appreciation to a *Kindred Spirit* when they encourage you. Our *Forever Family* are the connections who we need to thank for all they do for us.

I want to challenge you to take hold of God's promises in your life and join the team of encouragers.

Team of Encouragers

I believe in you. You are an encourager. Embracing all the Starting Nine Core Qualities is attainable and within your reach. Authentic encouragement draws us into loving and enjoyable relationships with others. Encouraging one another builds a new kind of community

Cultivating a team of encouragers starts with one—you, me, just one. There isn't a recipe for encouraging others, but we can begin with the love of Christ pouring out to others. Make it a discipline, praying for the Lord to put the person in front of you who needs a boost today.

Does encouraging others seem like a good thing but small in meaning? I believe it means the world to me when I receive a boosting word. I want you to think about someone who has made you feel you could accomplish anything.

Did their life-giving words mean little to you? What are the traits of that person you would like to emulate? That's how God wants us to be. I've never met someone who has received too much encouragement.

Pray that God will make you that type of encourager. Not all of us are cheerleaders, but we can learn how to respond rambunctiously to others' need for celebrations, even to those we don't know so well. Welcome to the team of encouragers.

Accidental Acquaintances

Accidental Acquaintances aren't usually in our lives very long, but we can encourage them with patience and kindness.

The first and third basemen are constant cheerleaders for the team. During each pitch, they talk up the pitcher and catcher. After plays, they celebrate with whichever player makes the play.

When an inning ends, they usually toss a ball into the stands to a young fan. They make contact with the person and intentionally throw it to them. The entire section near the young fan explodes in applause and returns a "Good job!" greeting to the player.

Being positive and using positive words toward these passing connections lifts them up. Look for the best in others, finding something we can point out as a compliment.

I love catching the eye of a mom at an airport who is juggling the kids, stroller, and car seat while dragging a blanket. When our eyes meet, I smile and nod. It's like a distant high five of "You've got this, Mama."

Sometimes, an opportunity arises, and I speak about the great things I see her doing. Inevitably, she smiles in response. "Good job, Mama" is always welcomed.

While at ballparks, I see many kids with dads. Many times, they look a little frazzled. Catching the attention of the kids to say how awesome it is to spend time with their dad at a game is a distant way to pat Dad on the back.

With *Accidental Acquaintance* connections, we usually don't use scripture to build someone up, but using the words of those scriptures can be a way to infuse God's love, and they don't even know it. "I am so impressed with your patience." "You are so kind."

If people are grumpy, one way we can respond to their negative attitude is to insert warmth with gentleness.

Each day, be conscientious to find someone we come in contact with to inject God's love straight into their heart.

Social Circle

The *Social Circle* is the group we can share more inspiration with. The outfielders are in a place to encourage the entire team. They yell words of belief in the players' abilities during plays. They provoke the fans in the bleachers to chant and cheer.

As a group of outfielders, they instill confidence in each other. They back up one another on plays while communicating verbally to keep each other safe and sharing information about positions during plays or numbers of outs.

After a win, they gather to do ritualistic jumps or handshakes to celebrate. Watch a Little League game, and you will see the kids replicating the celebration.

Some of these relationships allow for sharing how God works in our lives. With these connections, we offer prayer for any issues or concerns shared. They are primarily topical requests, but reassurance is given that they will be prayed over.

We must make a plan to uplift them. They are not close enough that we understand their strengths and weaknesses. But if we write down the things we notice, we can encourage them and remember to follow through when we see them again.

Sharing scripture is usually accepted when we are in the *Social Circle*. We can use verses to tell how the Lord works in our lives. We don't preach but use the scriptures as a foundation of God's actions in our lives or how we see God in theirs. These are more topical observations.

When we read a good book or see an interesting article that we think someone in this group would be inspired by, we tell them how it affected us. We may leave a message for one another on social media with an uplifting message or a comment or share on a post.

This connection may be part of a more significant celebration like a baby or wedding shower, a wedding, or a business accomplishment.

We aren't the planner in this group but are there to cheer on one another. Bringing cookies to a gathering to show our joy of being together is a nice gesture.

Kindred Spirit

Kindred Spirits are the connections where we are more understanding of their needs. The middle infielders are the heart of the defense. They assist each other in plays up the middle and in those double-play situations.

When a play is made, they celebrate with one another. They also chatter words of affirmation and confidence to other infielders, the pitcher, and the catcher.

They keep the outfielders in the loop by relaying information, number of outs, and encouragement. They also lead and direct the defense with positive communication.

Our *Kindred Spirits* are who we share the excitement of what the Lord is doing with. We also communicate how we see the Lord working in and through their lives. Growing together in the Lord, we live out the 1 Corinthians 13 love with loving and kind words that build them up. They communicate the same.

Thankfulness pours out between the *Kindred Spirits*. When we share issues, we are specific because we know the other will be positive and speak life-giving words.

Rarely are words life-draining, but if that happens, the other in the relationship will point them back to Jesus and redirect them to helpful encouragement.

Asking for prayer is a common practice. In this relationship, each person stops what they are doing to pray immediately with the person. The prayers are words of confidence and comfort.

When we see a book or article that would inspire or motivate them, we send it without hesitation. Kind notes are sent by text or even a handwritten gesture in a card that reminds us of them.

Encouragement can come in many forms, including supportive actions. Dropping off food, running an errand, making a call or sending text, or just checking in regularly can help boost them.

Forever Family

Our *Forever Family*, represented in baseball as the pitcher and the catcher, gives us an image of constant reassurance. The link between these two players is the momentum of keeping a rhythm of positivity to succeed on the field.

Seldom do they react negatively toward one another. It is their responsibility to keep the positivity. They believe that together, they can compete to win. They praise one another as they complete each at bat with an out, be it a strikeout where they need no help or any out completed by other players.

Forever Family partakes in an intimate level of optimistic reassurance. They think ahead and praise each other where they see faithfulness. When one is in a bad spot in life, they lift them with the hope of the future and what God can do.

They are each other's personal cheerleading squad. Struggles are shared, knowing the other will point them back to Jesus. When they need a boost, they know to go to one another. They naturally live out Christ's love in each other's lives.

Gratefulness is habitual for what the other has said or done. Sharing scripture through texts, calls, emails, or social media is constant. Prayer happens without being asked, and what they feel the Lord said about the other is communicated with excitement.

Forever Family knows how to celebrate. They clap loudly for all to hear whenever there is something to applaud. Everyone knows about all accomplishments, great and small.

Be aware of what they are doing and show up with cake and a confetti cannon. When we are enthusiastic encouragers, everybody wins.

We all pray for these types of people in our lives. Not everyone we meet will be our pep rally leader. We must be careful about who we assume will cheer us on and build us up. However, we need to be that person to everyone we meet.

Strong Sentiment

A warning when encouraging others. Make sure you maintain appropriate contact with anyone. I have to be careful because I am a hugger. Some people aren't fond of human connection. Ask for permission if you are unsure.

If you are someone who wants to freely share a word of encouragement, assess the person's ability to accept it before you overshare. Being considerate of others' boundaries and finding other ways to cheer them on is imperative.

Many people talk about, as I have in previous books, thankfulness journals. I want you to start an encouragement journal. Get a cute notebook or make a file on your computer. I like physical paper, but sometimes I use my notes app on my phone to avoid forgetting.

Begin with who has encouraged you in your *Forever Family*, then move to *Kindred Spirits* and *Social Circle*. List ways they have cheered you up or celebrated you. Then make a list of things you can do to be a cheerleader to others.

We aren't able to write down *Accidental Acquaintances* that we can bless, but what are some things this group has done to put a smile on your face or peace in your heart?

Also, make a page where you can keep encouraging scripture. What scripture infuses confidence in you? Write them down. Then when you find someone in need of God's word, you can share it with them.

Scripture can also be written in a note or text to boost a person who needs a bit of cheer. Loving others comes naturally when we are prepared with God's word in our hearts and minds.

I want to challenge you to become more encouraging tomorrow than you were today. I know you can, as you are already doing, but what more can we do as a team of encouragers?

Start by inspiring change for the better, then make it a reality. Take the first step to encourage and build others up in love. Advancing our relationships with others is the result of us exemplifying God's love.

We may not see ourselves as cheerleaders like the ones on the sidelines of sporting events, but I know we can inspire others. Stimulating others spiritually by sharing the love of Jesus through our words and actions and building others up inspires them to take that step of faith God desires. Continue to invest in the value of the people.

★ ★ ★

STARTING NINE CORE QUALITY #6

Compassionate

The world has become more compassionate for the rights of others, yet we also seem more self-absorbed. As a society, we are significantly more concerned with what we believe and need than our hearts are broken for others.

Compassionate means to suffer together, having or showing sympathy toward another's distress while having the desire to alleviate their pain.

Feeling empathy for someone's situation is the first step to having compassion and taking action to help them. There is strong motivation to change their issue or ease their pain.

Compassionate love shows sympathy toward another's distress while having the desire to alleviate their pain. To be compassionate, we must recognize the physical and spiritual needs of others, even if they overlook ours.

Loving others means putting down our concerns to stand in the gap. Giving and receiving compassion has a positive impact on our lives.

Again, we may believe different things or agree on many. Our judgment of how the people we disagree with got into their situation impedes our desire to help.

For instance, poverty is an issue that we know. We see people on the streets begging for money, or we experience kids in classrooms that dress differently or don't have money for lunches.

Quickly, we make assumptions or conclusions based on what we see. The man on the street begging is probably addicted to drugs. We don't want to give him money for his addiction.

The kid who has ragged clothes or doesn't have money for lunch—their parents must be lazy and not work.

The prostitute on the corner chose to do that. It's her problem, not mine. She could find a real job and get out of that situation.

We can very quickly say that's not our problem. However, by filtering people through the eyes of the Lord, our view completely changes.

The homeless veteran who has PTSD. Thank them for serving our country. How can we help them get the resources they need?

A child who sits next to our kid in school needs clothes. How can I help the school administrators get them clothes? Can we pay for their lunches?

The woman on the corner who's held captive by the man who told her he could help her make life easier. How can we help her see her value the way Jesus sees her?

We have opportunities every day to see someone through the lens of Jesus. Some are more apparent than others. We must look for what we have in common and how we can learn more about their situation.

Defense Strategy

Life is not easy, and often we grow defensive because we

struggle and don't want to be conscious of people's battles and pain.

When things are difficult for us, our hearts can become hardened. We throw up walls of defense to protect ourselves from hurt rather than open our eyes and hearts to see what breaks God's heart in the world. We must create a strategy to care for those things.

During the baseball season, I travel a lot. On each three- to four-day trip, I am in rideshares at least three times, if not more. I look at each ride as an opportunity to learn more about another culture or circumstance I may have yet to experience.

In the spring of 2021, I arrived in New York and requested a rideshare. When the car pulled to the curb, I loaded my bag and jumped in the backseat.

I said hello to the driver. He returned the greeting. The driver's accent indicated he wasn't from the United States, so I asked where he was from, and he shared his Middle Eastern connection.

The pandemic struck New York hard, so I asked how he had fared during it all. He immediately began to sob. This strongly built man was diminished to weeping while driving from La Guardia airport toward the city.

Immediately, my heart broke for this man. While I don't even remember his name, his story is etched on my heart forever.

When the driver gathered himself, he shared that he had lost five people in his home within a month. His mother, father, mother-in-law, father-in-law, and brother-in-law all passed from the virus.

The pain was palpable. Tears filled my eyes. I shared in his pain. I asked if I could pray for him. I was shocked that I asked. I assumed our beliefs were so different. But I was even more shocked when he agreed to allow me to pray.

I placed my hand on the transparent plastic partition that divided us and closed my eyes. I began to pray for the family, their pain, and that their hearts would be healed, in Jesus' name. While praying, I felt a thud on the plastic where my hand was placed.

It startled me, and I opened my eyes. I saw the back of his hand precisely as mine on the other side of the plastic. His tears were slowing.

I continued to pray for blessings and healing over them. When I was done, he thanked me for "praying to your God for my family." He said they needed all they could get.

I don't know if that man will ever believe in the saving grace of Jesus, but I do know that because of the compassion I showed toward him, he knows the loving, healing power of Jesus.

A Valuable Lesson

My personality can be big and sometimes hurtful. Once, I vocalized a comment to a baseball friend about how she was parenting her child.

The snide comment I gave was to get a giggle out of the group around us. I got the laugh, but it was a fiery dart of hurt in my friend's heart. I didn't know how deep the pain was until she wouldn't return my calls.

After, she avoided me. She sat with a different group at the Little League game and excused herself when I entered the bakery, where many moms gathered after school drop-off.

One morning, she said something very hurtful as she left the bakery. I followed her outside and asked what her problem was. Again, I wasn't very tactful.

Her returned tirade was hurtful, but so were my words earlier. I paused, took a deep breath, and asked her what I had done to hurt her so deeply.

When she shared my remark, I didn't see how that could be hurtful. But I chose to see it from her eyes. My comment was judgmental. I asked her if she could forgive me.

I saw the walls begin to crumble. I was grateful that my friend showed me compassion when I was critical.

It took a while to repair our friendship. I intentionally spent my time and energy feeding the relationship. I checked in on her and invested in helping her with her kids.

The comfort and patience I gave to her returned from her as she accepted my compassion for her. Her past was a burden she carried every day. We discussed the issues and prayed for healing together.

I could have checked this relationship off as too much work. Instead, I chose to manage my flaws and to comfort someone's pain I knew nothing about until she saw my love for her.

We knew our differences, understood where we were coming from, and forgave when needed. I learned a valuable lesson from my friend. Our relationship continues to thrive.

As I've spent time and energy feeding my baseball relationships, inevitably, some reciprocate the kindness and compassion and some do not. But that is not a reason to turn from being compassionate.

At every corner, we can see the physical needs of others if we genuinely look. Seeing the needs from God's perspective, not our conclusions based on our lack of experience in another's situation.

Spending time checking on, caring for, and investing in others adds value and clarity to our connections. Opening our hearts to share the pain and trying to help allows others to see the love God needs us to share.

Take the Risk

Being compassionate to others is risky and takes us out of our comfort zone. But as we become more aware of others' pain, God can open our hearts to love them.

Understanding their lives and perspectives while not

agreeing with them removes our judgmental glasses and gives us a glimpse of what God sees.

In all of the four relationships, we are called to love the whole person. Show compassion by fulfilling a physical or spiritual need when we have the opportunity with our *Accidental Acquaintances*. In our *Social Circle*, we must be grace-filled in our connections. We never know what another person is experiencing. Showing emotional compassion to our *Kindred Spirits* requires us to stop, listen, and be present with them. *Forever Family* is an ever-flowing river of tenderness and mercy.

Embrace the grace, love, and mercy Jesus offers, then pour it out to others.

Just As

"Be kind and compassionate to one another,
forgiving each other, just as in Christ God
forgave you."

Ephesians 4:32

God's compassion is that He sees our troubles and seeks to put them right. He asks us to be kind and compassionate in response to what He has done for us.

This is Christ's law of forgiveness, as taught in the Gospels. Jesus gives a startling warning about forgiveness. If we do not forgive others, God will refuse to forgive us. That's hard to hear. His forgiveness of our sins isn't the direct result of us forgiving others. But it is based on our realization. It is easy to ask God for forgiveness but challenging to extend it to others.

Peter asked Jesus, in the book of Matthew, how many times

we should forgive. The rabbis taught that we should forgive others only three times. Peter tried to be generous and asked if seven times was enough.

Jesus answered, "Seventy-seven times." Meaning we shouldn't keep track of how many times. We should always forgive those who are genuinely repentant, no matter how many times they ask. I thank God He doesn't put a number on how many times I ask.

Jesus also describes our need to forgive others in the Lord's Prayer. When Jesus taught His disciples to pray, he made forgiveness the cornerstone of their relationship with God. God has forgiven us, so we must forgive those who have wronged us.

Forgiveness Challenge

Forgiving others is challenging work. Many people would rather live in worry and pain than forgive others. We should never pray while bearing a grudge. It's seen as a tree sprouting leaves but bearing no fruit.

True faith changes our hearts. Real prayer breaks down walls of arrogance and revenge, filling the holes with love. If we are to pursue and seek peace, we must be aware of the need for forgiveness.

Jesus shows compassion to us by forgiving us. He also showed compassion and kindness in the physical and spiritual realms.

An expert of the law asked Jesus, "Who is my neighbor?" The question was concerning His command to love the Lord with all your heart and love your neighbor as yourself. Jesus told him a story.

A man was attacked by robbers when he was traveling to Jericho. He was left half dead. A priest passed him and did nothing. A Levite ignored his need. But a Samaritan saw him, took care of his wounds, and paid for a place for him to stay. Jesus asked which one was the man's neighbor.

The expert of the law couldn't even say the Samaritan did right. A deep hatred existed between Jews and Samaritans. He said the one who did the right thing was the one who had mercy on the man.

The Jews considered themselves pure and believed the mixed-race Samaritans were not. The man who asked the question thought the one who acted correctly wouldn't be the Samaritan.

Jesus saw the physical needs of people and showed compassion. When a large crowd gathered to hear His teachings, He realized they hadn't eaten for three days. He was concerned they might collapse when on their way back home.

The disciples were called to Jesus. They said they didn't have enough bread to feed the massive crowd. They only had seven loaves and a few small fish. Jesus broke the bread and gave thanks for the fish and told the disciples to distribute them.

In the end, there were seven basketfuls of broken pieces left over. Not only did God feed everyone, but He also provided more than enough. God sees the needs of people and provides in abundance.

He had compassion for the physical needs of the people, but Jesus ultimately came to bring salvation, our spiritual necessity.

Shepherd for People

Jesus was distraught over the spiritual condition of everyone He saw, including the spiritual leaders. They taught laws but didn't care for a person's whole being. Their refusal to believe in Jesus was an example of their stubbornness.

He came to bring salvation, and the Pharisees wanted to argue with him on trivial points of religious doctrine. They riddled Him with things like what is important and how to follow the law. They were obstacles to others being able to experience the kingdom of God.

Ultimately, they had Jesus crucified because of their single-minded attitude, neglecting what was necessary. They were proud of their ability to go above and beyond following rules but had no compassion for the people's spiritual needs.

Jesus continually fed His flock with parables and teachings that fulfilled the laws on which the Pharisees stood firm. He went through all the towns and villages, teaching in the synagogues and proclaiming the good news of the kingdom. He healed diseases and sicknesses.

Jesus tells us about the final judgment in Matthew. He says He will separate His obedient followers from the pretenders and unbelievers. Our faith is real evidence of how we treat all people as if they are Jesus. That's no easy task, but we must emulate the compassion of Christ.

He was the shepherd for the people, bringing more workers to expand the kingdom and leading them to God.

Caring for Others

No one will ever be perfect here on earth, so we must accept and love other Christians despite their faults. We must carry each other's burdens and point them back to Jesus.

When we see faults in others, we are to be patient and gentle, like Jesus—comforting them when they are heartbroken and strengthening them when they are weak.

People are hurting all around, us included. Isaiah prophesied that the coming Messiah would be despised and rejected. A man of suffering who would be familiar with pain.

One of the places we read about Jesus being emotionally moved to tears was when He saw the people crying after the death of His friend Lazarus. He was deeply moved in spirit and troubled.

In Luke 19, Jesus wept when He approached Jerusalem. The Jewish leaders rejected the Messiah. They refused God's offer of salvation through Jesus. God didn't turn from the people who obeyed Him. He continues to offer salvation to all people.

Jesus showed great compassion for everyone who was troubled. He understands our pain and wants to help every person in need.

When we fail to be compassionate, we are not personifying the love of Christ. Being aware of God's compassion toward us leads to understanding how we are to offer sympathy toward others with a desire to alleviate their burdens.

Caring for others is central to how we are called to love others. Our love is based on our faith in Christ, but not limited to it.

Shepherding others is a necessity for our *Accidental Acquaintance* connections. It can be extremely challenging to offer forgiveness when we feel wronged in our *Social Circle*, but leading by example shows others how it can be achieved. *Kindred Spirits* and *Forever Family* are the relationships that build our base of caring and help us learn how to share it with others.

God has chosen us to be kind and compassionate. By forgiving others and taking care of their physical and spiritual needs, we personify the compassion of Christ.

Compassionate Christian

Being a compassionate Christian requires being more like Jesus every day. Asking the Lord to break our hearts for the things that break His is a great prayer for each morning.

We are incapable of accomplishing this on our own. The only way is with the Holy Spirit guiding and leading us to be more empathetic.

God is gracious and righteous and full of compassion. Compassion is the product of us being holy and beloved. Not conforming to what others are doing but being transformed into the image of Christ.

God has chosen us to do good work for Him, and that work starts with our hearts and minds. Forgiving and showing mercy to those who are in need physically and spiritually.

We learned about empathetic listening as a tool for being selfless. Take that a step further in putting action in our hearts to open them to feel empathy for others. Develop our eyes to see others as God sees them.

Compassion starts with putting our opinions aside and letting our hearts feel the fullness of other people's suffering. It is connected to what we do.

Accidental Acquaintance

Accidental Acquaintances are the group in need of the most compassion from us. Not knowing much about these people doesn't initiate compassion toward their burdens.

The first and third basemen show empathy from a distance, as their interactions are few and far between.

Carrying each other's burdens is challenging when the contact is distant. However, they are sympathetic when the other doesn't make a routine play. They are aware of the other's struggle to retire a runner. They understand the feeling and do not impart judgment quickly. They get it.

Forgiveness has to be given when significant plays occur. With their empathy for their respective positions, they usually have no hard feelings about not completing a play. They know they could be next to "boot" the ball.

The fault in *Accidental Acquaintance* relationships is that it is easy to judge others when we know little about them.

Differences in opinions and religious or political beliefs

cause a great divide in this group, not showing empathy for the person but judging their views.

Our world is full of hatred and accusations. Being compassionate is not natural for many, especially on social media. But I've also seen it in airports, ballparks, and city streets. Condemnation and accusations are easily thrown. Racism and cultural differences are still alive.

As Christians, we must view others through the lens of God. Be aware of anyone different and try understanding their likeness in Christ's view. Put yourself in their shoes. Show mercy.

Try to understand their life and perspective. Our goal is to understand and be empathetic. Even if you disagree with them, do not negate their feelings. I'm not saying to condone sin, but our words of awareness and understanding are small gifts of God's love.

When we see people standing on a different side of belief, we give generous measures in our thoughts. Pray for them, not with judgment but with empathy and mercy.

At every corner, we can see the physical needs of others if we genuinely look. Understanding the needs from God's perspective, not our conclusions based on our lack of experience in their situation, opens our hearts to care for them.

A compassionate Christian should be on the lookout for ways to meet the needs of destitute people. If they are thirsty, give them a drink. Hungry? Provide a hot meal. Finding a way to open our hearts and hands serves the person and God.

Spiritual needs are a bit harder with *Accidental Acquaintances* but can be discerned when our hearts are ready to see their pain. Taking time to talk and listen helps to open our minds and spirits to be humane and have tender feelings toward others.

When people are distraught, we encourage them. If someone believes differently than us, we open our hearts to share the story of how God has transformed us.

Social Circle

Social Circle relationships are a bit easier to be aware of the physical and spiritual needs of others. But some don't share the needs until you move into a deeper connection.

The outfielders in baseball have each other's and the infielders' backs on many plays. During the game, their communication and encouragement are necessary to work together. Their concern for one another creates a seamless action during plays.

The compassionate nature of the outfielders is visible after a win. They often come together to hug or do a ritual handshake celebrating the victory.

In a larger group we are in contact with more regularly, we can assess their needs if we desire to see them. Physical needs are apparent, but it takes more work to comprehend their spiritual needs.

Empathy doesn't come naturally for some; we must work on it. For those of us with extremely soft hearts, we must regulate the deep feelings we have when others are hurting.

When we are in closer contact, conversations may venture into places of disagreement. Because of our expectations or assumptions, we can take them a bit too far.

When we share our beliefs, there should be no judgment. Ask questions about the reason they think the way they do. Listen. If you need to be challenged to be aware of the needs of people in this group, join a new group to listen.

We should never try to prove people in this group or anyone wrong to make ourselves right. Fighting our selfish ambition permits us to open up to our differences.

The most compassionate thing we can do for many, especially our *Social Circle*, is to let them know you see them. Being aware of them and the help they need shows you care.

Work hard to be considerate. Listen to what they need to share. Continuously pursue an understanding of where the other person is coming from.

Forgive them when there is a grievance, even if the relationship doesn't grow or if the forgiveness is not accepted.

Spiritual needs may not be shared in this group, but we can share how God's compassion toward us has changed our life. The connections may grow into a deeper relationship when compassion is shown toward them.

Kindred Spirit

Kindred Spirits get each other on another level. They are connected to each other's needs. This is a group where being compassionate to one another results in mutual mentorship.

The shortstop and second basemen are the baseball example of compassionate mutual mentorship. They provide resilient assistance, being the heart of the diamond.

They commiserate about plays that didn't happen and celebrate each other when they complete a double play. The two players communicate with each other and are sympathetic to other players who aren't playing very well.

Kindred Spirits are honest when we've done something wrong. Accepting each other's shortcomings is vital to this level of relationship. They don't allow weaknesses to be their focus because they know we all make mistakes.

It is easier to be compassionate at this level. Forgiveness is fast. Mercy and grace are shown without judgment. They share in God's forgiveness and pray for one another when needed, even if they aren't asked.

Their feelings are more tender for each other when they see the other serving from their heart. They share information so they may understand each other better.

Physical needs are known and met before they express the necessity. Spiritual needs are met when they pray with and for one another, even when things are good.

Forever Family

Compassion comes extremely easy for *Forever Family* because of their deep love for one another. They serve one another's needs without question.

Pitchers and catchers are gracious and kind to each other because of their deep connection. Their understanding of the different needs comes naturally. The partnership is responsive and aware of the need for empathy during games.

When one is not as strong as the other, they do not judge but step out to discuss the problems and agree on how to proceed.

We understand that we are holy, chosen, loved, and clothed in compassion, so we care deeply. *Forever Family* doesn't judge. We discuss problems and show mercy when there is a difference.

Together we serve others and one another. We talk freely and really listen to what the other says.

Physical needs are never ignored and met before they go too far. For *Forever Family*, serving others is top on their list of activities.

Spiritual needs are shared, and continual growth is shared within this relationship. Serving others with the love of Christ is our goal. When compassion is shown, it makes an impact on others.

Compassionate Heart

In each relationship group, we must be creative in how to be compassionate. As we know, it is easier to be aware and understand the differences in some and more complex in others. Some need something out of the ordinary when we are empathetic to them.

Compassion is connected to what we do every day in small acts. Caring for others as our hearts are broken for the things that break God's.

Fight the beast of resistance to care for and love others with a compassionate heart. Be an advocate for someone you may not know. Volunteer for an organization that exposes you to things you've never before encountered. Show that you value others as you show tender humanness.

Accept the forgiveness challenge and make sure each person who needs forgiveness is covered in prayer and forgiven. Forgiveness for ourselves is also included. Being a shepherd of love allows us to show kindness naturally, continuing to care for the betterment of the people we are in contact with each day.

Begin each day praying for God to fill our hearts with compassion, being His hands and feet to the community of people He desires us to love. Then, take action when someone is in need.

★ ★ ★

STARTING NINE CORE QUALITY #7

Respectful

Many believe showing respect is admiring someone or being sensitive to their feelings and rights. Respect is the foundation of caring and honorable behavior. It is the bedrock of loving relationships.

Being respectful is when we care enough about another person to consider how we impact them. The heart of respect is caring. Respectful love cares enough about another person to consider how our actions impact them.

All humans deserve respect because they are made in God's image. We aren't supposed to find the famous more important than someone less renowned.

It doesn't mean ignoring differences or tolerating people. We should care enough to accept the significance of our differences but look beyond them and respond respectfully.

We must first find our footing in our self-respect. If we cannot value and appreciate who God has called us to be, we will never be able to show others they are essential and needed.

Healthy relationships grow when we see ourselves the way God sees us. A healthy view of ourselves shows others we value who God has created us to be.

Self-respect is not falling to the world's idea of how we should look but submitting to the truth of who we are in Christ. God knows us and still loves us.

Showing ourselves respect according to God's view allows us to open up to giving that same respect to others.

To disrespect others is to disregard who they are as humans. To react to Christians this way is dishonoring part of the body of Christ. For unbelievers, we fail to show them the love of Christ alive within us. Disrespect is rude and causes harm to relationships.

I was taught as a child to treat others how I wanted to be treated. I looked at it with foggy views of wanting to treat some well and others not. As my faith life grew, my idea of honoring others changed. I had to break habits I held.

Zero tolerance for disrespect should be our meter. Look for differences to embrace. Celebrate the unique distinctions and show respect to them.

Being Better

When we started our professional baseball career, I was the age of the wives and girlfriends of the players.

Let's just say, thirty-seven years later, they remain in the same age range, and I've grown thirty-seven years older. The relationships I've been blessed to grow along with have challenged me to become a better servant of the Lord.

From the young girlfriend who tentatively walked into a spring event to a girlfriend of a scout just getting into the crazy life of baseball, I have loved and cherished the knowledge we have shared. Younger to older. Older to younger. The path of learning goes both ways.

Parenting presented the greatest slope of the learning

curve for me. Raising kids in a professional sports environment is a challenge in many areas. My goal was to teach our boys to see each person as equal, no matter if they were the superstar of a team or the janitor cleaning a bathroom on the concourse.

I also had to keep myself in check when meeting famous people. Early in our career, I was starstruck by authors, actors, and other sports stars who visited our team.

One time, a man ventured into our family room at the ballpark. A few of us watched from there to avoid walking through the crowd at the end of the game.

We were all startled by the man's appearance. His hair stood in twelve different directions, and his facial hair growth was uneven. The red- and black-checked, half-tucked flannel shirt hung from one side of his dingy jeans.

The girls quietly nominated me to find out who he was and why he was in our sacred space of the family room. I ventured outside to the clubhouse door security, Joe. I inquired about the scruffy man. Joe chuckled.

When he told me who the man was, I was shocked. Someone as famous as him shouldn't look so disheveled.

Returning to the family room, I introduced myself to the gentleman. He responded kindly with a twinkle in his eyes. I proceeded to make introductions to the other women in the room.

He sat with us on the couches, and I began to batter him with questions about his books and where he got his ideas for each.

The conversation continued, and we didn't even realize the game had ended. Running from the babysitter, my boys shot into the family room like a cannon, asking if they could see Dad. I was so enthralled with the author that I was rude to my kids.

They left the room without me knowing, only to be stopped by security at the clubhouse door because the coaches were meeting. When the kids came back again, I barked at them for interrupting my conversation.

One of the boys voiced his irritation with me on the drive home. He was rude but called me out on how the man was more important to me than they were.

At that moment, I realized I treated my kids terribly because of a conversation with a New York Times bestselling author. From that time forward, I put myself in check.

I began to treat each person I encountered with respect intentionally. I did it initially, thinking I would teach my kids, but the Lord revealed how much I had to learn. My kids once again trained me.

Showing Respect

Respect is a significant element of healthy relationships, with those we are close to and the ones we temporarily encounter. My first goal was to see each person's value, regardless of status.

When I entered ballparks, I took time with the people working the gates and security to look them in the eyes. Rather than ignoring others, saying please and thank you drew smiles and at least gave a tug at the corner of their mouths.

The boys and I would stop by the customer service booth to say hello to the man who had worked at the ballpark for over fifty years. He sat on his little red stool and chatted with the boys. He got updates about school and whatever sport they were playing.

Then, we headed to the concession stand, where two ladies asked some of the same questions. They gave big hugs and kisses on the cheeks, sending the boys into giggles about how gross it was that they'd gotten smooched.

As the boys and I entered the clubhouse area, we stopped and said hello to Joe, pausing to inquire about his family or the day's happenings.

We ran into coaches and players in the hallway to the family room. Hugs and questions again, but we took the time.

It wasn't always easy to take the time to show respect to others when the kids had been fighting in the car on the way to the ballpark, or when they just wanted to play with friends. I had to be intentional.

Invested Interest

Loving others takes deliberate actions. Many times, it was calculated to show the boys how to act, but then it turned into a genuine concern to show others respect.

As my oldest son, DJ, stood talking to a starting pitcher for our team, Mr. John walked into the clubhouse hallway. Mr. John was a custodian who emptied the trash cans on the concourse near the clubhouse.

When he approached, my son ran from the player to hug Mr. John and tell him about his latest outing as a pitcher for his Little League team.

The player asked my son why he didn't share that information with him. DJ said that he hadn't asked.

DJ valued Mr. John because he invested in his interests when the player talked about his game or what DJ did during the game. Respect for others isn't about the outward value but also the inward significance of having love for others.

Being respectful to other wives and girlfriends in baseball has opened up opportunities for me to learn and teach my kids. The age difference doesn't mean that I deserve more respect than them.

Respect stands upon the other core qualities of loving others. We are being respectful by seeing people's value, treating them with dignity, and appreciating them for whom God created them to be. However, we don't always know how to treat each other respectfully.

Our pride may not allow us to when we don't think someone

has earned our respect. When there is conflict, it doesn't come naturally. Or we don't know how to be respectful.

Respect for the people we encounter is a product of learning the other core qualities. The ones most closely related are compassion and encouragement. Seeing others as God sees them, not judging them for their circumstances, helps us connect with *Accidental Acquaintances*.

Using good manners connects us with all of our connections. In *Social Circles*, make sure eye contact is maintained. Address mistakes quickly with *Kindred Spirits* and *Forever Family*, playing fair and never causing harm.

As Christians, we live a life of integrity and consistent, uncompromising devotion to strong moral value. As a result, we will respect others, showing them they are worthy and honored.

Do to Others

"So in everything, do to others what you would have them do to you, for this sums up the Law and the Prophets."

Matthew 7:12

Jesus spoke to crowds on a hillside near Capernaum. It is called the Sermon on the Mount. The sermon probably covered several days of preaching but spans chapters five through seven in the book of Matthew. He challenges the proud and legalistic religious leaders of the day and us today.

When Jesus comes to the portion to teach about asking, seeking, and knocking, He tells us to persist in pursuing God. He proceeds to speak to the crowd about the heart of God. He is not selfish, begrudging, or stingy. He is a loving Father who understands, cares, and comforts.

Then, Jesus taught what is commonly known as the Golden Rule. In many religions, it is stated negatively. But Jesus made it more significant by saying it positively—treat others how you want to be treated.

It is not always difficult to hurt someone when they've hurt us. But it is much more challenging to take the initiative to do something good for them.

The Golden Rule Jesus taught is the foundation of active goodness and mercy. The kind of love God shows us every day.

It is a simple yet impactful way to say we should respect the dignity of our fellow humans. God emphasizes the high value He has for humanity early in the Bible. Doing unto others is the minimal viewpoint we should take toward everyone.

Each of God's children demands valuing and measuring worth by His standards. He calls us to go beyond the minimal—to go above and beyond to show others how much they are loved.

Disrespect Shown

Showing disrespect to others can cost us relationships. In 2 Samuel 10, King David had been friends with another king named Nahash. When David heard his friend died, he sent a delegation to express his sympathy to the king's son, Hanun, who succeeded his father.

David wanted to show the kindness to Hanun that Nahash had shown him. Hanun's commanders said they believed David was spying on their country to overthrow it. Hanun misread David's intentions.

His men seized the envoys and disrespected them by shaving their beards and leaving them half naked. His actions humiliated the men and insulted Israel. Rather than admit his mistake and ask for forgiveness, Hanun spent a lot of money to cover up the incident. It cost him more than money.

Disrespect brings on trouble in relationships. Because Hanun was overly suspicious and judged David for previous issues, he brought disaster upon himself. While we should be cautious if someone has dealt unfairly with us before, we should not assume every action is ill-intended.

In the following chapter of 2 Samuel, we learn that David's men completely destroyed the land of the Ammonites, Hanun's people. His disrespect for David caused great pain to everyone involved.

Integrity

Respecting others is based on integrity, the inner commitment to truth. After Jesus' baptism, He was full of the Holy Spirit. He left Jordan and was led by the Spirit into the wilderness. The devil tempted Jesus for forty days. Jesus showed integrity the entire time Satan tempted Him.

For Jesus to fully understand the human experience, He had to face temptation. He had to undo Adam's work. Adam had been created perfect, yet he gave in to temptation and passed sin on to the whole human race.

Jesus resisted Satan. He is the perfect example of integrity. He was entirely God and fully man, yet He respected God's teaching and Himself as a man avoiding temptation.

Satan tested His beliefs when Jesus was at His weakest in the desert. Jesus used scripture to counter Satan's attacks. We must also resist the devil's attacks by having faith in God's promises. Integrity relies on scripture to battle sin.

Jesus stood firm in His moral values throughout the battle with the devil. He showed amazing uprightness by standing on God's word and His character. People who walk in integrity walk securely. It guides us and provides a blessing to generations to come.

Living God's Character

We must learn to live out God's character to be respectful to others. God is a God of justice. We must act with what is morally upright or good—being fair and righteous in our love for people.

God is **good,** and we are called to live out that goodness. He has given it to us as a fruit of the Spirit. God is good not just once but all the time. When we seem to be fighting the devil in our circumstances or with others, we must cling to the truth that God is good.

God is also **holy.** Holiness is our goal in respecting people, especially those we may disagree with or who haven't earned our respect. He understands our needs, cares for us, and comforts us when we are discouraged.

When we live out the character of God, we can respect the **dignity** of others. Dignity is respect for ourselves and others.

Embracing dignity increases respect for ourselves. Self-respect is not equal to selfishness. It is the understanding of who we are in Christ. Regarding who He has created us to be.

Then we can provide the respect they deserve because they are made in the image of God.

Loved.

Cherished.

Celebrated.

Forgiven.

We are to accept ourselves the way the Lord acknowledges us. The same as we are called to love others. We are all made in the image of God and worthy of love.

Showing respect to value their dignity is living out the characteristics of God, believing we are all valuable. We pour out goodness without judgment. We are to respect them even if they've not earned it, treating them as we want to be treated.

Expectations to Act

Peter tells his readers in 1 Peter 2 to submit to the civil author-ities, the Roman empire, who were cruel tyrants. He wasn't advising them to compromise their consciences but to live according to the law of their land. He says to show proper respect to everyone in everything.

This is an example of respecting authority and others even when we are in conflict, suffering, or don't believe the same.

We are given specific instructions from Jesus not to judge nor condemn but to forgive and give. He says that whatever we measure others by will be the quantity we receive.

God expects us to act with respect toward others. Putting other people's needs on par with ours is loving others the way Christ commands.

The Bible shows many examples of how God accepts us and how we should acknowledge others. Jesus was also a perfect example of accepting others, no matter their sin or choices. He extended grace and concern to many. We are called to do the same.

Accepting and loving as God does doesn't mean we accept destructive behaviors. We are to be careful in allowing them to enter our lives. However, showing respect to the least of these is mandated.

Treating others as we would want to be treated is the foun-dation of our connections with *Accidental Acquaintances*. Continuing to live God's character through our lives leads us to grow our relationships with our *Social Circle*.

Kindred Spirits show each other dignity and see what God is doing in and through each other. *Forever Family* remembers kindness to each other and challenges us to show that to each connection.

Respect isn't earned—it's given. Given in godly portions without holding back, caring for others' well-being without needing theirs in return. Only because our respect comes from the Lord as we live our lives with integrity.

Advocates of Christ

Disrespecting others is to devalue those whom God has created. To do so to believers is dishonoring a part of the church body. To a nonbeliever, it is unloving and doesn't show that Christ lives in us.

Respecting others is a reflection of God's love. We are different and called to love others distinctively. God values life beyond measure. When we respect others, we are living out the character of God.

We often forget how to respect others when we are constantly confronted with someone harsh and hurtful. Being disrespected by someone close to us, we build fortified walls around us.

I must remind myself to respect all of God's people, no matter the treatment I receive. I have no control over others' actions, only self-control.

The fundamental ways to be respectful of everyone are to be kind, courteous, and polite. Basic manners of "please" and "thank you" let people know we value them.

Accidental Acquaintance

Accidental Acquaintances are the group we must remember to appreciate and show consideration to. They are a group we can pass by and not even notice. Instead, let's begin to notice and acknowledge them.

The first and third basemen show appreciation to each other

when plays are independently completed. They see the bigger picture of the value of each player on the field.

They may not be in direct communication as many of the other players, but they are part of the team.

Respect for *Accidental Acquaintances* is when we accept everyone, even though they are different from us or don't agree on social topics.

If we look at every human as part of God's team, we respect them for who they are. Treating people with dignity means we treat them as worthy. Respect the boundaries others place in their lives and those we create so we can honor them.

Sometimes Christians can be judgmental toward people who do not believe as they believe. My heart breaks when I see very verbal Christians shouting that God hates individuals because of their sins.

God doesn't hate individuals. Jesus embraced many people deep in sin but never said He hated them. God despises sin, not the person.

When we accept people who may be in a different season of life, have lower or higher economic standing, or choose evil over faith, we love one another as Christ has commanded.

Showing respect to this group is being an advocate for Christ. Speaking up for those who cannot speak for themselves.

Respecting God above all else, not joining in their choices, but letting them know they are made in the image of God. And for that, we are thankful.

Exhibiting patience and kindness shows recognition of their dignity. They may not treat us as we would like them to, but we, as God's children, treat them as we would like to be treated. Sometimes just sharing how valuable they are in God's eyes can redirect a disruptive conversation.

Each person we come in contact with brings value to our connection. If we meet someone in passing, a smile and a word of encouragement are a way to treat them as valuable.

In our power, we cannot have patience for people who don't reciprocate respect, but with the Holy Spirit, we love anyway.

On one of David's and my vision trips to a third-world country, we were invited into the home of a young mother. She told us how honored she was to have us in her home and gave us little cakes she had made. She asked if she could pray for us as we finished our visit.

Her prayer was filled with thanksgiving and protection for our travels. She was pouring out all the love Jesus could offer to a group of people she might never see again. The young mother was an advocate for Christ. We were encouragers for her life.

Social Circle

Our *Social Circle* usually creates a level of topical mutual respect. It is shown for those in an authoritative position in the workplace, the church, or another social setting.

The outfielders constantly communicate and work together. Their level of courtesy is based on the hierarchy of the center fielder being the captain of the outfield.

The specific responsibilities of the outfielders are honored by each of the players. They accept each other's positions and particular tasks.

In our *Social Circles*, we dig deeper into getting to know one another. If we are comfortable with ourselves, we invite others closer.

Taking an interest in one another allows us to know whether we can deepen these relationships. We help others get to know one another and become more informed on their differences. Starting discussions about our lives helps us learn about our differences without assumptions.

Be a role model for the people in your volunteer or work groups. Show them how we value our beliefs and how we respect theirs. We cannot demand respect for our values if we don't show them we honor their viewpoints, not agreeing but listening with care and concern.

The people in this group are the ones with whom we don't freely share our burdens. We listen to anything they have to share. Our respect toward them is not to share their issues with anyone else.

We listen and keep it simple in our responses to honor their feelings and needs. They don't need to know everything we are thinking.

Respect among the *Social Circle* is not always given freely. The connection can grow deeper if they are vulnerable and generous with their relationship.

Kindred Spirit

Kindred Spirits take responsibility for honoring others. They treat each other with kindness and consideration.

Both of the middle infielders forge respect for the abilities of the other to be able to work together. Their activity on the field is respectful, as their movements during double plays allow the others to be authentic to their responsibility for the play.

Their partnership works well because they admire each other's quality of play. Their expectations are based on the admiration they have for the other.

With our *Kindred Spirits*, it is appropriate to challenge their disrespectful behavior. A level of mutual respect is expected at this level of connection. It involves understanding each other, our differences, strengths, and weaknesses.

We flourish on our common grounds of values but don't shy away from challenging each other. Our boundaries are respected, but we inspire each other to grow.

We care deeply for one another and are concerned with our impact on each other's life. We respect how each other desires to be treated—different than *Accidental Acquaintances* and *Social Circles* because of the mutual response.

Being careful not to damage our relationship is paramount. When we disagree, we do so with kind words.

Express gratefulness for who they are in our lives. We admire one another and give more than we get in our relationship.

We preserve promises we extend to one another because making promises doesn't ultimately give respect. Keeping them does.

The people in this group are the ones with whom we can share our burdens. We obey the limits of distributing our information to others.

These connections respect you for acknowledging their personal needs, not sharing their issues.

We can listen to them without dumping our issues on them immediately. *Kindred Spirits* know they will have an opportunity to add to the conversation when appropriate.

Our responses to one another are honest and encouraging. We don't have to fix their problem, nor do they need to improve ours. Most of the time, our respect is shared.

Forever Family

Our *Forever Family* makes it easy to treat them as we want to be treated because they mostly do. Respect is common and mutual in this connection.

When we hear interviews after games from the pitcher or catcher, we understand their extreme respect for one another. The batterymates maintain their integrity and uplift each other. They battle for each other during and after the games.

They are confident in themselves and the relationship they hold with each other. Investing in one another's growth and success is their gameday habit. They give each other more than any other player on the field.

Our *Forever Family* holds our utmost respect. Going beyond giving more than we get, we outdo one another with honor. We are truthtellers laced with grace and mercy to one another.

We model behavior with one another that challenges us to lead others in a positive direction of respect. Keeping each other's promises because we wouldn't dare go back on one.

Investing in our *Forever Family* is our primary duty of honoring who they are to us and how much they have invested in us. Be honest but tactful, while continually pointing them back to Jesus.

They fight the good fight for one another on critical issues. And are "extra" sharing admiration for each other when they speak with different connections.

When there is a plan to get together, they are either on time or early. There is an understanding of the importance of the time they sacrifice with family or work to get together.

Acknowledging that when we've gone too far or done something disrespectful, we immediately apologize. We are messy people, even as *Forever Family*.

Remember, with all of these connections, feelings matter. Be mindful of what we say and how we say it.

Silence isn't always a great thing when someone needs to be heard. Always smile. Sometimes a smile can turn someone's whole day around. Showing them the love of Christ through our respect is paramount to building loving relationships.

Advocating for others shows our respect by treating them how we would love for them to treat us. If we strive to live out God's character, we will present Christ-like behavior, appreciate others as holy beings made in God's image, and respect their dignity.

Mutual respect can be built with each of these contacts. It's based on understanding our differences and still loving. Showing others their significance, meaning, and purpose will point them to Christ. We are advocates of Christ.

★ ★ ★

STARTING NINE CORE QUALITY #8

Trustworthy

Trust is a crucial element of loving relationships—being trustworthy must be a priority when building loving relationships.

Trustworthy means to be able to be relied on as honest and dependable. Trustworthy love pours out dependable, reliable, and honest character.

When I began to write this section, I got stuck. I couldn't quite grip the concept because of pain from the past. I was fighting memories of broken trusts. I reached out to my Facebook community and asked two questions.

What has caused you to lose trust in a person? And what are the qualities of someone you trust? Their responses were helpful.

The feedback was both profound and heartbreaking. The leading cause of losing trust in someone is lying. Some individuals lie to us without concern about how it affects us when the truth is discovered.

People also lie about us, making false claims about us,

tearing us down, and hurting others' views of us. One person shared that they believed these lies were based on pride.

Next, a break of trust happens when a person shares confidential information about us. Let's say you share with a friend that a person's comment offended you. They go to that person and share what you said.

Some shared church hurt affected them—something many of us have experienced when someone in the family of Christ breaks our trust. Trust is fragile.

The cornerstone to stability, transparency, and respect, being trustworthy takes commitment. When we dedicate ourselves to being reliable and dependable consistently, we choose to be accountable for what we say and do.

We had someone dear to us betray our trust. This individual took advantage of our generosity and love. Lies and deceptions were covered up with more untruths.

They used Bible verses to pray for others' misdoings. They blamed others, but I found out their blame pointed in the wrong direction. They never admitted they had lied.

Our trust was broken. I didn't think I could ever trust anyone again. If someone close to us hurt us this way, what were people who weren't as connected to us doing?

Being cautious became my go-to. Making assumptions and accusations when people hadn't done anything became my response.

People Hurt

Many of us have experienced hurt from people we are close to. Quite a few of them were within the church.

We can find people who do not show this quality at every turn. Many in the public's eye have been dishonest and irresponsible. Their actions make us want to retreat and doubt everyone.

Connections that deceive lack integrity. They don't stick to their values and beliefs. Others can form our lack of trust in our lives, or we can learn to take cues from the habits of people we can count on.

The people who choose to be honest and responsible help us grow our personal quality of trustworthiness.

Trust is destroyed when we feel someone belittles us or speaks to us with contempt, lacking respect. Harm occurs when we feel betrayed.

When we drop a priceless vase that shatters into a million pieces, we assume it could ever be repaired. It may never be the same again, but we can replace it with another.

When our trust is mishandled, it feels broken beyond repair—but God. When we depend on God, we can be the person who builds trust with others and with those who have torn our trust.

Diverse Opportunities

Being trustworthy relies on truth—God's truth and honesty to one another. It gives our connections a safe place to feel understood and protected from harm. It is a place where we feel protected.

In our first year of professional baseball, David was a rookie ball manager. The majority of the team were young Spanish-speaking players.

Thrown into situations that were not normal for them, many had never flown on a plane. Most knew no English. There were the issues of being in a hotel with running water and working toilets. The modern conveniences we never think about were new entities in their lives.

The young men were making more money than their families made in a lifetime. It shocks me when I say this because, at that time, players were making very little in rookie ball.

They couldn't open bank accounts on their work visas, so they would go to check cashing shops, which took a large percentage of their check when it was cashed. Players would wire money home so their families could eat. They sacrificed for their families.

Our hearts broke for the players in a new country with little understanding of the language and the lifestyle.

We took time to invest in them, helping and loving them. Being reliable, we built trust with them through mutual respect, and our baseball family grew.

Loving those young men grew when we lived in some of their countries and saw the struggle of everyday life.

Fast-forward many years, our middle son is a mental skills coach. He speaks Spanish fluently and works with players new to the U.S. With his understanding of the players' countries and cultures, they depend on him for guidance.

As a parent, I am so proud of Charley. He looks out for the good of the Spanish-speaking players. He listens and is cognizant of their feelings while being honest and encouraging them to overcome obstacles and succeed.

Being confident when we communicate with others exemplifies our trust in the Lord. We can count on Him one hundred percent of the time. When we put our trust in God, we can trust ourselves. He is the only one who never lets us down because He always has our good in mind. Jesus is perfect. People are not.

We can have faith that we can make it through any situation. When we are aware of our thoughts, it helps us lovingly express them.

The assurance that we are there for someone cannot be underestimated. Speaking words of truth with grace reassures others that we have their best interest at heart.

The Great Recycle Bin

Baseball is a giant recycle bin. We're all thrown in the recycle bin and picked up by another team. We often work with staff members we've previously encountered. If we are in the game long enough, we repeatedly run into the same people.

Sitting outside the clubhouse, a player approached, staring at the ground. The veins in his neck bulged, his lips pursed, and his face red. I called his name, and he turned. "I didn't see you."

I asked if he was okay. He shook his head aggressively. I patted the metal bench beside me, and he sat.

He began with accusations and assumptions about a coach who had scolded him for how he played that day. I let him vent for a few minutes. He raised his hands and growled about the experience and his desire to confront the coach.

Once he finished, I asked if I could share something with him. He shrunk on the bench and looked me in the eyes.

"Buddy, don't burn bridges. This game is a big recycle bin. You will see him again. If not this year, then maybe in a few. God's got this. Be the man God needs you to be."

A few years later, I ran into the player on a back staircase of a stadium. He now worked in the front office of a different team.

After we hugged and caught up on family news, he said, "I want to thank you." He reminded me of our conversation and how it had helped him be accountable to others in the game.

Sure enough, he was working with the same man he had vented about years earlier. "He's not that bad," he said as he shared about them working together. "I'm so thankful I didn't burn that bridge.

When we encounter people who break our trust, it breaks our hearts, but it shouldn't change our view of doing good.

Turning rivals into allies happens when we love others, beginning with integrity and honesty. To be trustworthy finds favor with God and people.

As believers, we are accountable to Jesus. People will come up against us. We have to be self-controlled and not do anything that would go against God.

Showing trustworthiness to our *Accidental Acquaintances*

requires us to embrace diverse opportunities. Rely on truth first in all of our relationships. In our *Social Circle*, we must remember to be consistent and remember we are all part of the big recycle bin.

Be consistent in our honesty and care for our *Kindred Spirits*. Always keep promises and be honest with our *Forever Family*.

Trustworthy people make the world a place where God is seen. These connections in our lives are important. But we need to be an example.

Nothing Bad to Say

"Similarly, encourage the young men to be self-controlled. In everything set them an example by doing what is good. In your teaching show integrity, seriousness and soundness of speech that cannot be condemned, so that those who oppose you may be ashamed be- cause they have nothing bad to say about us."

Titus 2:6-8

Paul wrote to Titus, a Greek believer who stood before the church leaders in Jerusalem as a living example of what Christ was doing in the lives of Gentiles. Titus was a trusted travel companion and one of Paul's closest friends. Paul had devel- oped Titus, over time with special care, into a mature Christian and responsible leader, doing good for the sake of the gospel.

People flocked to hear Paul's teaching. He knew he needed help to encourage, discipline, and teach the churches when he was gone.

So he trained young leaders to take on this task. His letter to Titus was a step in the discipleship process.

Most likely, the lessons he emphasized in the letter were many of the ones he taught Titus. Here, Paul writes about how to become trustworthy. He emphasizes encouraging young men to be self-controlled. The advice was essential in Greek society. The men believed at that time that being a husband and father was a functional role, not a nurturing one.

They neglected the responsibilities they should have had for their families. Men who are good examples of Christ by caring for their family's needs are important role models. They needed to learn to say no to ungodly and worldly passions.

Paul encouraged Titus to be an excellent example so others would see and imitate their good deeds. Being reverent, not slandering others, and teaching what was good would have a more significant impact than his words.

He told Titus not to criticize people when he taught God's word. Studying the Bible and listening before speaking helps present moral uprightness.

Paul said to be pleasant and worthy of respect, sound in faith, love, and endurance. He urged Titus to make the teachings of God attractive.

Because of Titus' honesty and righteous ways, he couldn't be condemned. The people who opposed him would have no proof. A good life is a witness to the gospel's power.

Throughout the book of Titus, we see Paul's trust in Titus and vice versa. The discipleship process begins with trust between the two involved, each being trustworthy.

Trusting God

To be trustworthy, we must first trust God. Proverbs tells us to trust the Lord with all our hearts. It also gives us great advice on how to do so. We do not rely on ourselves.

When we depend on God, we surrender our knowledge and rely on His plans. We find in scripture that He is dependable, reliable, and consistent. The Lord is totally incapable of being anything less than trustworthy.

Crying out to the Lord happens when we surrender all to Him in response to our trust in Him. Prayer is our avenue for our cry to Jesus. Through prayers, we turn over our control to Him.

We must trust God, but did you realize He trusts us too? God entrusts us with the gospel. He sent His Son for the forgiveness of our sins.

God doesn't want us to keep that information to ourselves. He trusts us to share His love with others.

A person who trusts in the Lord is like a tree planted by the water, surviving when there is a drought. Its leaves are green, and it continues to bear fruit. We, too, flourish when we trust God.

In the Old Testament, Joseph was arrogant in his youth. He learned humility and wisdom through his experiences of being enslaved and imprisoned. His life was not simple or without trouble, yet he continued to work hard.

Joseph trusted God no matter how difficult his life became. He had a gift of interpreting dreams and would decipher one for Pharoah. Joseph's wisdom was so great that Pharoah put him in charge *of all* of Egypt. In foresight of the famine, he stored grains.

When his brothers came to Egypt to acquire grain so they wouldn't starve, it was their brother whom they'd sold into slavery who saved them.

Joseph trusted God through it all and became the one who saved the twelve tribes of Israel by using God's wisdom and gifts.

We are entrusted with the talents and gifts He gives us. If we have a gift of singing, only harmonizing in the shower would hide the blessing. Wisdom given by God is to be shared to help others draw close to Him.

A dear friend who can counsel with understanding and knowledge of God's word travels worldwide to help others in traumatic situations. God trusts her to share.

The gift of speaking the word of God, sharing His love, and being someone who can be trusted are all talents that God gives us.

When someone betrays us, we get angry. In that rage, we question God. Our trust in Him and people fails. The life of Joseph shows us that we should continue to trust God through all of our struggles.

Continue to do the right thing, using the gifts God has given us, and strive to be trustworthy so that God can continue to use us to shine His light through us, being dependable and consistent.

Paul used Timothy as someone with the qualities of a trustworthy person. He had seen Timothy in action, and Paul believed him worthy of respect and reverence for God's word.

Timothy came from a godly family. His mother, Eunice, and grandmother, Lois, were Jewish believers who taught him about Jesus. Timothy became one of Paul's closest companions and pastor of the church at Ephesus. He faced all sorts of challenges from the church and the community. To encourage him, Paul sent two letters.

In the first letter, Paul gives fatherly advice, urging Timothy to hold onto his faith in Christ. He goes on to teach about training ourselves to be godly. Godliness has value for all things—instructions against false teaching and how our spiritual life becomes nourished through the word and prayer.

Counted On

Being an example for others in speech, conduct, love, and faith are the habits that build trust from others. We must be reliable, consistent, and dependable so that others can count on us.

To become more trustworthy, we must stand up for our

belief in Jesus—following our consciences and relying on God's word to grow in wisdom and knowledge.

Trust can grow when we consistently have the courage to do what is right. Being sincere but candid presents a spirit of vulnerability in our actions.

He desires us to connect with our *Accidental Acquaintances* by living out His truth. In our *Social Circle*, we must emulate His holiness by taking no part in gossip or other sinful activities.

With *Kindred Spirits*, we are to be the same, day after day glorifying Him in our relationships. *Forever Family* continues to live in His wisdom and understanding of our connections.

God is trustworthy and trusts us with what will bring Him glory. There are no excuses for believers not to grow in our responsibility to be trustworthy.

Being Trustworthy

When I inquired on Facebook about the qualities of a trustworthy person, the first response was honesty, telling the truth even if it hurts and being transparent.

Then they shared other qualities like being who they say they are, being consistent, and keeping information confidential.

Learning the ways to love others by being trustworthy begins with honesty. Truth, even when it may not be received well. But the truth is told to show the other person that we can be held accountable.

Living with integrity shows others we are who we say we are. Sometimes words build us up to a point where we can never fulfill expectations. Keeping it "real" builds confidence in one another.

Trustworthy people are dependable. We keep the word of another. Things told confidentially should always remain confidential unless abuse or harm happens to that person.

A person is vulnerable when they ask us to pray. Taking that prayer to the Lord is the only place we should go. Prayer requests should be included in the keeping of confidence.

Authenticity shares our true character with our contacts. Be yourself because everyone else is taken. God has created us to be who we are, not what we think others may want. We learn to show trustworthiness in each of the four relationships.

Accidental Acquaintance

Accidental Acquaintances usually don't have enough time together to build trust. We determine if we will rely on someone for temporary help by how we perceive them.

On a baseball field, the first and third basemen size each other up on each play where they interact. Will they cover the ground needed to help with a bunted ball? A bunt is when a hitter shortens his swing to softly hit the ball and dribble it down the first or third baseline.

If the ball trickles up the middle, the first and third basemen equally hustle for the ball. They decide who will back off and make the play during that time. They listen for cues and ensure they keep the other player safe, trusting each other's decisions to make the play.

People we are in contact with in passing should see our integrity in everything we do in public. We embody our values, build bridges that unify, and are sincere.

Trustworthy people protect the most vulnerable, making them feel safe. A positive attitude toward them shows them the joy of the Lord.

Doing what is right is at the top of our hearts with *Accidental Acquaintances*. We show empathy and are respectful.

The mom on a plane, an older adult having trouble crossing

the street, and a rideshare driver having a bad day—all are opportunities to show kindness.

Giving our full attention to people we are in contact with helps them feel comfortable. Keeping our ears open to listen to their stories, making eye contact, and responding in love. Kindness counts.

Asking them about their life allows them to test how we respond and what they can share. Usually, there is not enough trust to share deep thoughts, but I've seen it happen.

It amazes me how often I begin to ask topical questions, and the person pours out their heart to me. God's love, through me, allows them to open up.

Social Circle

Our *Social Circle* is the area where we can begin to build trust. In this group, we can try new things even when it's hard. Again, honesty is vital.

Baseball outfielders contribute to each other's plays. They build trust by backing up each other when the fly ball is going to one specific player in the outfield. They trust the player will catch the ball but are there for backup if needed.

They support one another in the entirety of the outfield grass. The center fielder, being the captain of the outfield, takes on the responsibility of covering the majority of the middle portion. They show the other players they know they can catch a ball by backing off of plays in their territory.

Being an example in speaking, behavior, love, and faith is our goal in being trustworthy in our *Social Circle*.

In this group, our yes is yes, and our no is no. We do what we say we will do and complete the task. If we are given a deadline on a project, we meet that commitment.

We create opportunities for others to shine to show others we are trustworthy. Contribute to projects without wanting any kudos. Self-control is part of being authentic.

If God has called us to a task, there may be others who are already serving. It doesn't mean there is no room. He will make a way.

Supporting others is a clear sign to these connections that we are reliable. Showing up on time and being consistent show them we can be counted on.

Confidentiality is an essential trait in the *Social Circle*. Telling others' secrets, even when wrapped in "Let's pray for them," is gossip.

Kindred Spirit

Trust is developed more with our *Kindred Spirits* than the *Accidental Acquaintances* or *Social Circles*. We tend to give ourselves wholly to them.

The second baseman and shortstop are the heart of the infield and are trustworthy to the other players on the field. They are loyal in supporting the other players on plays and ensuring they have the information they need during innings on the field.

They keep secrets well. When a runner is on second, they communicate without words when they are trying to catch him off base, catch the throw from the pitcher, and get him out. They are clear in their communication and acknowledge when there is a failure.

Transparency, being who we really are, plays a large part in being trustworthy with our *Kindred Spirits*. We are certain they will love us anyway, so we are vulnerable at a deeper level.

Honesty reigns at the top of our connection. Communication is better at this level. We share our current concerns and are open about our emotions.

Kindred Spirits support one another by sticking to what they say. They have upstanding reputations that confirm their trustworthiness.

They are a safe place even when we fail. Gratitude is

abundant, and loyalty leads. Making time for one another, they drop everything when the other is in need.

Forever Family

With *Forever Family*, we trust without verifying. We believe in them even when inconsistencies happen or they seem too unbelievable.

The pitcher and catcher trust beyond measure. They have the deepest level of trust on the field. The pitcher relies on the catcher to call a game for success. They depend on them to frame balls thrown, so they appear to be strikes if they are close in the zone.

They hold each other accountable for the best outcome on the field. The trust deepens when a pitcher throws a perfect game, a no-hitter, or the catcher uses the pitcher's performance consistency to make reliable pitch suggestions. They count on each other.

We care deeply for our *Forever Family*. There is a sense of security that goes beyond comfort. They are fully trusted, and gossip about the other in this connection never crosses the lips.

Strict information boundaries are set, and secrets are kept. Confidences are never compromised.

There is no question about who they turn to when they have a need. We entrust one another with our prayers. We protect the gospel in our relationship and share our talents and abilities.

Forever Family trusts in the Lord, are trustworthy, and maintain the trust of one another. Transparency is respected so that we know we can always count on them.

If any hurts happen, quick repentance happens. We regret the wrongdoing, confess our mistake, and keep our promise never to let it happen again.

Fears are shared with the confidence that the other person

will respect them. We are who we say we are, and our actions prove that to them.

They stand by and protect. Trusting our *Forever Family* more than any other connection results from our dependability.

The connection of trust relies on our faith and how we live that out with this connection. The joy of the Lord penetrates our relationship, trusting Jesus first and then each other in response.

Looking out for one another and being conscious of each other's feelings, fears, and struggles help build trust.

They follow through in keeping our word and keep promises. Their actions match their words.

We can only be trusted when we have gained the trust of others and they begin to believe in us. Then our connections grow.

Trust Phrases

Three words I learned later in life helped me build trust in relationships, from the concession stand worker to my family. Those three words were **"I don't know."**

Too many times, I felt like I needed to have all the answers. I don't. None of us do. I've habitually acted like I have all the answers to Bible questions.

When I began telling those who asked questions that "I didn't know but would find out," they trusted my answers more than they did when I had a quick response.

Another phrase that rebuilds trust when hurt is **"I was wrong."** Earlier in my life, saying I was wrong allowed others to take advantage of me in times of weakness. Learning to trust the Lord would take care of me, I began using this phrase, which allowed others to trust me.

When we have the quality of being trustworthy, we can grow loving relationships because they see how we have changed and their confidence in us grows.

Trust is fragile but a crucial element of loving relationships. Be who God has called us to be so that no one has anything bad to say about us.

The importance of being trustworthy cannot be underestimated in loving relationships. It takes honest communication and integrity.

It doesn't mean we're perfect, but it does show others that we love God enough to love them. Building trust is a daily commitment.

As we follow the teachings of the Bible, we are an example for others. Using our spiritual gifts and blessing others, being diligent in our faith, and being thankful allow others to see we are dependable.

Trusting God is the bedrock of our ability to be trusted by others. Being consistent in our care and honesty in our relationships, we strengthen the connections we have. When we build trust, we are able to share our faith and what God has done in and through our lives.

Not everyone will believe, but they will have nothing to say against us if our intentions are good.

★ ★ ★

STARTING NINE CORE QUALITY #9

Generous

God is the most generous in dispensing love. As we have gone through the first eight of the Nine Core Qualities, we've directed our Christ-like love to others. The core quality, generous, begins with God's overwhelming, never-ending love.

My friend, God loves you. He created you in the womb. Every detail, each hair on your head, and the spirit within you started there.

No matter the circumstances of your birth or the outcome of experiences over the years, you are unique, special, and loved by a mighty God. He makes no mistakes.

We were made to glorify Him in everything we say, do, and think. Our generous God is ready to pour all of His love on us. Open your arms wide and receive all that He desires to give you. God's generosity is the overflow of His love and goodness. Being bighearted is the result of His kindness.

It's here for the taking. Receive it at its fullest.

Our usual understanding of generosity is showing a

readiness to give more than necessary or expected. Being abundant in love is when love comes from the center of who we are. Generous love gives more affection and tenderness to others than is necessary.

Our baseball lives can be messy—much of our everyday life can also be messy. In our messiness, we find a place where God calls us to love one another. No matter what we have experienced, He asks us to love others as He loves them.

I can't count how many women I've been in contact with in baseball. From the wives and girlfriends of players, coaches, and front office employees to those who work the ballpark security. Then, there are the many fans we have encountered over the years.

The generous spirit of love exudes from many, but some take more than they return. I hope that as we've learned the different levels of connections, we can be free to love, while also discerning the profoundness of each relationship.

We express our generous nature through our time, talents, and resources by prioritizing the hours in our day to serve in the gifts God has given us in our spirit and with the material items we possess.

Giving and Receiving

When I talk with people about being generous, they often go directly to money. Our finances are a place to be helpful. God calls us to tithe and give. What one person may be able to provide, another may not.

Giving money comes from the understanding that it's not ours anyway. God provided our income, so we are to share that revenue.

I know from experience that giving when we don't have much is terrifying. The first year David had a big-league coaching position was our marriage's poorest financial and spiritual year.

The salary he received didn't cover all of the expenses. We rented an apartment in the city where he worked while paying a mortgage elsewhere.

Then, the taxes were doubled because of living and working in different states. I had no clue there were dues to be paid to the clubhouse attendants, so our budget took a hit.

By the time we got our checks, our bills were barely covered. Many nights, the only food I had was what was left over on the boys' plates.

We were in a difficult place financially, and it was a burden on our marriage. To think I needed to give anything out of the few dollars left over for food and gas was too much for me.

Giving was nowhere in my vocabulary. Spending time with people who lived generously taught me I had more to offer than I knew.

A rookie wife on the team was one of the most generous people I had ever met. She spent time with people, acting as if they were the most interesting people in the world.

She paused with purpose as she came in contact with each person—her intention was to show them love.

Her arms were always filled with a hug or a small token of love—a piece of candy, a card of encouragement, or even a rock were shared to show her care and concern for them.

One veteran wife on the team invited everyone to the playground at her apartment and provided snacks for the kids and coffee for the moms. The funniest part was bringing her coffee pot with all the condiments to the park. She said it was cheaper that way.

She was extremely generous in her financial giving to organizations where her family was involved. She knew where it was essential to invest the money and was not stingy.

I learned that what I had to give at that time was my time. I helped other wives with their kids when they needed extra hands. Holding babies was and is my specialty.

I also had a talent for hospitality. I hosted Bible studies at my house with an invitation to bring a snack. I served water. The coffee pot wife brought a can of coffee and the condiments. I provided a safe place to gather and share.

During this time, I had to learn to accept help when offered. I was good at helping other wives with their kids, but when they would offer to help me, I wasn't good at receiving.

It was my responsibility to take care of my kids. I didn't want to put that burden on them. It took a friend's stern assessment of me to shake my thoughts. She told me I was taking away the opportunity for her to serve God.

When we say no to others' giving spirits, we may hinder where God has asked them to serve. Learning to accept help wasn't easy, but once I did, the blessings I received in the giving were immense.

Sharing Experiences

Another year, a fellow wife was a fantastic teacher of the Bible. I sat listening, rather than trying to ensure all the kids were okay and the food was displayed on platters. I received the greatest gift of knowledge and wisdom from God's word.

Spending time with people who live with a generous spirit is an excellent way to learn generosity. Taking time to be in the presence of those in need helps us see how we can give more than necessary or expected.

David and I have traveled with Compassion International to the Dominican Republic to see their programs in local churches. It changed our view of extreme need and how we could help.

Another messy part of the baseball family includes health issues that come when least expected. Many times, a test result or diagnosis comes during a game. Our family room becomes holy ground as we gather around the one who received the news or experience.

During a game, one of the wives jumped up from her seat, looking ghostly. She handed me her toddler and didn't say a word. She sprinted from our section.

Just days earlier, she shared that they were pregnant again. She was a little nervous about the timing but overjoyed about the news.

My heart dropped, thinking about what may be happening. When she didn't return, a few of us walked to the family room. There she lay on the couch sobbing. We gathered around her. Words weren't needed.

We laid our hands on her, someone holding her hand, and one of the women began to pray as the tears fell.

Some sobbed uncontrollably, afraid or thankful that it was not them. Prayers continued as the Spirit sat gently on the heart of each woman.

When we were done, conversations were light as we all processed in our way. She sat on the couch in the arms of another.

When the game was over, we lingered in the family room as husbands began to appear.

The sweet girl who received the bad news went to the clubhouse, as many stayed with her kids. I went with her for support.

Her steps were slow as she began. Little by little, her shoulders went back and her head up. As we approached security, she was ready to share the unbearable news with her husband. She collapsed in his arms as he stepped out of the double doors.

I walked beside her during this experience because I knew how she felt. I'd lost babies too. Pouring generous love onto her when she was in need was all I could do during this time. It was enough.

Spreading Love

Being generous in love is when our attitude directs toward love. We can overflow in the love God has poured into us, ready to give more than necessary with our time, talents, and resources.

When Hurricane Maria devastated Puerto Rico, Pittsburgh Pirates players, coaches, and the front office collected more than 450,000 pounds of supplies for the affected people.

It was an honor to be part of the group and see the city of Pittsburgh come together to pour out love to the people in Puerto Rico.

The goal was to fill one cargo plane with supplies. They exceeded their target, doubling the donations. A very generous couple with the team donated the money to charter a second plane. The generosity of everyone exceeded expectations.

If you can give, give—support, support. Donate, donate. Commit to being generous.

Dispense love freely to *Accidental Acquaintances* just as they are, because of God's love that lives in us. Generously overflow love and goodness to our *Social Circle* to show them the generous love of God. Giving and receiving flow freely between our *Kindred Spirits* and us. With our *Forever Family*, our shared experiences overflow with spreading love to one another and others.

God is generous in His love for us. In response, we are generous in love with others. I pray each day we continue to ask, How can we be more giving today?

Serve Humbly in Love

"You, my brothers and sisters, were called to be free.
But do not use your freedom to indulge the flesh;
rather, serve one another humbly in love."

Galatians 5:13

Christ died to free us from sin and a long list of laws and regulations. He loves us so much that He came to set us free. Not free to do whatever we want because that would lead us back into slavery to our selfish desires.

We can now do what was impossible before. We can live unselfishly and not be stingy. Our service to others isn't to earn God's love and favor but to share His love.

Love for others and God is the response for those who are forgiven. His forgiveness is complete. Whoever is forgiven much is loved much.

Paul distinguishes between freedom to sin and freedom to serve. A license to sin is not freedom because it binds us to others' corruption and sinful nature.

Christians should not accept sin because we can do right and glorify God through loving service to others.

Spiritual freedom delivers us from the power and bondage of sin so we can serve the living God and His people. It is freedom from legalism and the control of the flesh so we can experience Christ.

Let's live a thank-you life and a want-to life rather than a have-to life, being thankful for a relationship with Christ rather than being bound by law.

The creator of the universe, the almighty God, loves us so much. He cares about our lives and wants to be part of it. He wants us to serve humbly in love.

In Galatians 5, Paul writes about the fruit of the Spirit: love, joy, peace, patience, kindness, goodness, faithfulness, gentleness, and self-control.

He says the work of the fruit is spontaneous work by the Holy Spirit. In us, the Spirit produces the character traits found like Christ. We cannot obtain them by trying to get them without His help.

We must know, love, and imitate Jesus to allow them to grow

in our lives. The product of the Spirit-filled life is in perfect harmony with the intent of God's law.

When we exhibit the fruit of the Spirit, it fulfills the law far better than someone who is without love in their heart but follows the rules.

Grace of Generosity

Choosing to be led by the Spirit and living our lives motivated by God's Spirit compels us to love generously. When we steward generously, we find purpose.

We are the beneficiaries of the goodness of God. Every spiritual blessing is through our relationship with Christ. Encouragement to live out His love for others propels us to live openhanded and openhearted.

God provides what we need when living openhanded in giving our time, talent, and resources.

Jesus could not have shown compassion to the crowd when they hadn't eaten for days without a boy with five small barley loaves and two fish. The boy and the disciples didn't think it was enough, but Jesus made it enough.

We must cooperate with the Holy Spirit to cultivate and grow in the grace of generosity, generously giving the love and forgiveness God so well offers.

Pouring out to others the love of Christ is living in the overflow of all He has done for us. We show that Christ loves us and others as we open our hearts and hands.

The Corinth believers excelled in everything. They had faith, good preaching, great knowledge, and much love. Paul encouraged them in 2 Corinthians to also excel in the grace of giving.

The stewardship of money often is given a different status in our discipleship than in other disciplines. Many believers want to grow in faith, knowledge, and love but stop short of monetary giving.

Growing in the mature use of all resources should include giving. God can provide the desire and enable us to increase our capacity to give.

Generous Restitution

The Romans levied taxes on all the nations they controlled to finance their great world empire. The Jews opposed the tariffs because the taxes supported the secular government and their pagan gods.

Tax collectors were among the most unpopular people in Israel. Some Jews by birth chose to work for the Roman government and were considered traitors. It was understood that tax collectors were making themselves rich by taking advantage of their fellow Jews.

People were uncomfortable when Jesus went to the home of Zacchaeus, a tax collector. Despite the facts, Jesus loved him. Because of this love, the despicable Zacchaeus was transformed and set free.

He went from being a cheater to giving to the poor and making generous interest restitution to those he cheated—Zacchaeus, serving humbly in love.

Zacchaeus demonstrated inward change with outward actions. Generosity is a sign of a transformed soul. The gospel opens our hearts and our hands.

God loves a cheerful giver. Giving gladly frees our fingers to loosen the grip of our desires to store up our treasures on earth.

The Bible contains over two thousand verses about money, tithing, and possessions—more scripture than those that discuss faith and prayer.

Money is important to God. He gives it to us and expects us to give back. Jesus spoke a lot about it because He knew it was a heart issue causing people to give up on him or not follow.

We never see a trailer of money and possessions following a hearse. We cannot take it with us. A knowledgeable financial advisor friend tells us he hopes our last donation is one to empty our bank accounts when we die.

In our four relationships, we must be cheerful givers, showing each God's love by loosening our grip on our gifts and treasures. Gracing our *Accidental Acquaintances* by serving them humbly in love. Emotional generosity to our *Social Circle*, including them in outward actions of partnering with them in sharing all that Jesus has done for us.

Kindred Spirits share the generosity of goodness toward one another. *Forever Family* shows generous connections, spiritually, emotionally, and materialistically together.

Whom will we serve? I choose God and His love for others.

Openhanded Generosity

Openhanded people give freely and kindly if it's with time, talents, or resources. Being generous in love, we create a lifestyle of generosity.

Pray that the Lord will give us wisdom and knowledge. As we begin, ask the Lord to lead us to unselfishness and where to put our faith into action, allowing us to be free and kind.

Accidental Acquaintance

Accidental Acquaintances allow us to generously love some people who may have never experienced God's love.

The first and third basemen are generous with supporting other players on the field. Since their plays are primarily independent, they aren't as beneficial to others on the field when involved in the majority of the plays on the field.

They cover their assigned base and receive the balls for crucial outs in the inning. Each player benefits the team by being willing to stay out of plays where they shouldn't be involved but giving the play to the outfielder behind them or the players on the infield in the middle.

Being generous starts by paying attention to *Accidental Acquaintances* and their needs. Have a conversation with the people we come in contact with each day. Very quickly, we can pick up on their need for help.

Each year we are approached by hundreds of organizations to participate in a campaign or to give to a specific goal. It took us a while to understand that we didn't need to feel we had to donate to everyone who asked.

I felt guilty that I couldn't help the hundreds of ministries and other organizations that do amazing things. Praying for wisdom, David and I choose who we will support each year.

Many organizations and people we encounter may have needs, but we must make decisions based on our connection and their trustworthiness.

Sometimes the way we give to others is in our time by volunteering and spending time with others. When we volunteer, we are placed in front of many who need help. Giving hope and sharing compliments and genuine kindness opens our hearts and hands more.

With each encounter, we can give people the benefit of the doubt by asking questions, listening, and responding with kind words. Make them feel welcome and speak positive words of Jesus' love.

With our *Accidental Acquaintances*, we are generous when we give more than asked and when it doesn't make sense. We do this when we give up a seat on a plane when a family isn't sitting together.

Walking through the grocery store, I often see women who are much shorter than I am. I volunteer to get the item on the top shelf they need help to reach.

As a teenager, I worked in a nursing home. So many lonely

people sit in a chair all day without a visit. I began to take extra time to listen to their stories. Oh, the memory lanes they walk down when given a chance.

Spontaneous generosity only takes the desire to do it. Each day, we can find places to spread love abundantly to those we come in contact with.

Social Circle

Social Circle generosity is based on affirmation, a lending hand, and thankfulness. This group of relationships is encountered when we take the step of volunteering and participating.

The outfielders' interactions are abundant in affirmation. They are supportive and encouraging of one another. They provide backup on plays and are confident that other outfielders will be there to help them.

The center fielder covers the most ground to get to a ball in play. They have a strong arm to make difficult plays and give more than expected in each play they are involved in.

The corner outfielders constantly communicate with the center fielder and lend a hand when needed. Gratitude is a language shared after plays.

Our *Social Circle* is the group we meet when volunteering or participating in group activities. These can also be our neighbors who we take time to help when needed.

Elderly neighbors may never ask, but we can see their grass getting tall and take extra time to mow. A mom with a new baby and a few little ones may need a helping hand or a box of diapers.

The meal train at church is a great way to be generous. Sign up, make a meal, and take it to someone on the list.

Hospitality is my love language. I love to host events large and small. It is also a way to network with others. During the baseball season, I love to host picnics in the park so we can all get together and learn more about one another.

Including people who may not be in our inner circle allows them to make new friends and connect more profoundly. Be welcoming and share in knowledge and wisdom.

When we see someone with a talent to share, we connect them with the organization, group, or person who needs that quality. I love to connect people who have the talent to share with others.

One way to be generous is to send a handwritten note to someone when you see them shining or send a quick thank-you for something they've done. When we see something and generously say something, it speaks love.

Kindred Spirit

Being a humble servant is an opportunity to serve those who may not expect it. It helps build relationships with them. Some may be an opportunity to grow into *Kindred Spirits*.

In our *Kindred Spirit* connections, we profusely give praise and time. Our talents are shared by helping and uplifting them.

The second baseman and the shortstop are at the heart of the field and considerate of all players. They share information and give praise consistently. Getting out of the way of one another for the other to succeed happens during double plays.

They share thankfulness for help when a runner tries to steal a base. They are willing to be the heart of the defense, being involved in every defensive strategy with the rest of the team. Advice is given while also celebrating the success of the team.

Kindred Spirits hug often. They share their success with celebrations. Special events and victories are equally festive, and they are generous with their love for one another.

A special quality of generosity is carving out time. They listen without distractions, admit when they are wrong, and know what boundaries not to cross.

Openhanded generosity involves teaching each other skills. They make meals for one another even when not asked.

My *Kindred Spirits* are an exceptional crew. I love buying cards with a special message and writing encouragement inside. A young mother new to the big leagues struggled with the tremendous change from the minor leagues and needed a little love.

I found a card with a funny message and wrote in colorful capital letters, "You've got this, Mama!" I slipped the card into her diaper bag so she wouldn't see it until she got home.

I received a text from her late that night. She was so thankful and told me the words on the card helped her take a deep breath and know she could make it.

Generously praising one another helps build confidence and courage. We never regret it when we lavish loving words on someone.

Forever Family

Forever Family showers generosity on each other. Prayer is poured out even when it isn't requested. Appreciation abounds.

The pitcher and catcher have a relationship that accepts the generous character of the other. The link between the battery-mates is acceptance and sharing of talents. The catcher may be the same every game, but the pitcher changes. No matter the lineup, the two players make it happen.

Partnering up to face each batter lends opportunities to help each other. Advice is given and received for the betterment of the team. Their wisdom abounds.

Our *Forever Family* also carves out time with one another. Plans to hang out are a priority. Spontaneous generosity to one another happens regularly.

They are also a team that pours out love to others. They volunteer together, making a more significant impact. Their time is prioritized to help, and talents are shared between them. They encourage one another to use them where they are most needed.

They tend to be openhanded in secret. No public announcements are made about their generosity, but they know it about one another.

Appreciation is boundless. They celebrate each other's accomplishments and successes with high fives and praise. Hugs linger as they speak words of encouragement.

I give my undivided attention when I spend time with my *Forever Family*. Phones are silenced and put away.

We forget where we put them because our time is precious with each other. Celebrations are unending, constantly looking for how to help and offer appreciation.

Sometimes it's hard for us to accept our *Forever Family*'s generosity. When they offer to help, we frequently say no. Not because we don't need help but because we'd rather be on the giving end, not the receiving. We have to purposefully allow others to help.

Openhanded

Being openhanded in generosity can be difficult when we're asked to give outside of our tithe at church.

As a steward of God's money, we are responsible for giving. However, we must be responsible for discerning the places we give.

Here are a few places to find information about giving and some reputable organizations where we can serve humbly in love. The list isn't exhaustive but is instead a guide of how and where to find and discern where to give and serve with one another.

- Compassion International
- Fellowship of Christian Athletes
- Baseball Chapel
- Professional Athlete Outreach

- Pittsburgh Kids Foundation
- Urban Impact
- Path2Freedom
- Coming Alive Ministries
- Truth in Sports

Find somewhere or someone with whom you can share generous love.

Serve humbly in love. Share all that God has done for us. Show others God's glory through all that we do. Live in a posture of openhanded generosity.

★ ★ ★

SIGNIFICANT IMPACT

"The adults are talking" was my first negative experience with a fellow baseball wife, but not the last. I had to decide to retreat, respond, or reenter with a new attitude.

We all have a choice when it comes to the people around us. Being hurt is unavoidable.

- Awkward situations will arise.
- Introverts will retreat.
- Extroverts will chase.
- Sometimes everyone shuts down.

Committing to loving people, which we didn't choose, mandates tough skin. I will never advocate staying in a relationship that is abusive or degrading. However, we need to commit to the process of building.

In baseball, we have a new group of young women, wives or girlfriends of the newer players, each season. Some were there the year before, but the turnover is high among players and coaches.

We've spent nine seasons with a team, while with others,

we've only spent one. Many organizations trade players between them, so we see them on different teams.

As I stated earlier, baseball is a big recycle bin. We are all thrown in, shuffled around, and pulled out in a different city on yet another team. Some players and coaches go up and down from the minor leagues to the majors and to other organizations.

Most baseball organizations have four to six minor league teams. Some players and their families can see a few different levels in one year.

Many baseball wives and girlfriends have become friends, and quite a few have built deeper relationships. Like all other friendships, some were easy, some took more work, and some never developed.

In each encounter, I had to choose to invest in the person to draw closer to them. Some took me far out of my comfort zone.

Complicated Routes

On teams, players' interactions happen in the clubhouse, but a different connection develops on the field. Considering the game of baseball and how the players have played for so many years, one would think the connections would happen seamlessly.

It doesn't always happen that way. Sometimes complicated routes occur. When a new player arrives, it can be a bit uncomfortable. It takes time for things to run smoothly on the field and off.

They need to get to know the other players and the coaches—feel out the way the team plays together, what works and what doesn't. Language barriers cause some to feel awkward.

In our first year in baseball, David managed a rookie ball team, the first step in the minor leagues in the US. Our team had kids from the Dominican, Venezuela, Puerto Rico, and a few from the States.

I took on the challenge to converse with a translation book (no cell phones with translation apps back then), which created many mess-ups with unending laughter. Many players were intimidated by the thought of trying to speak English.

Some kids could not read, so the book didn't help. I began to notice how they would retreat from the group of us sitting on picnic tables in the baseball cloverleaf (where multiple fields are connected).

We tried to encourage them to join in, but they stayed at a distance. Little by little, the hesitant players would sit on the edge of the group and laugh occasionally. Then, I brought food. Food always breaks down barriers!

Their response began with one or two words, just enough to break down the awkward feelings of the language barrier.

Winter Ball Turkey

David managed or coached in winter ball for eleven winters. The season extends from October through January (February if you go to the Caribbean World Series). We were in Venezuela for three winters and the Dominican Republic for more than eight.

In our first year of winter ball in Venezuela, I felt like the rookie ball boys who walked away or stood on the outskirts of the Spanish/English butchering-of-language sessions. I found myself in a country where only a few spoke English.

We needed to speak Spanish if we wanted to eat. Adventurous translations of foods on menus challenged us to try things we may not have chosen otherwise. Let's just say, full-size green beans and pieces of corn on a pizza would not have been my first choice.

We stuck it out and tried many new things. Because I took risks rather than complaining, the Venezuelan players and families began to spend more time teaching us Spanish.

As American Thanksgiving Day approached, I told David

I wanted to cook for the team. Many of us lived in the same building in the center of Caracas.

I found a butcher shop in the mall downstairs from our apartment. Juan, the most boisterous of the butchers, was always ready to help me with my Spanish.

During my first interaction with him, I pointed to a chicken breast and asked, "Como sé dice eso?" How do you say this? He grinned from ear to ear and said, "Chicken." I retorted back, "Not in English!" It broke the tension of my feeling self-conscious about not knowing the language.

Juan greeted me as I entered the store almost two weeks before Thanksgiving. I believe the other butchers were afraid to look at me. I might speak English, which frightened them.

I pulled out my handy translation book and asked if he could get me a whole turkey. "Yes, yes." He spoke in broken English without hesitation.

We hashed out the weight I wanted and when I needed it delivered. I wrote a reminder in my paper calendar (remember this was "back in the day") and returned to the apartment to put the boys down for a nap before the game.

I returned on the day Juan and I had agreed on the delivery of the turkey. When I entered the shop, Juan greeted me with a hearty "Hola!" All the butchers turned to face me. Juan hurried to the back. I knelt to hush the boys from arguing over a toy and heard a loud thump!

To my dismay, when I looked up, Juan flopped a limp turkey on the counter. Feathers, feet, and all! Something failed in translation. After a few more turns with the translation book, Juan agreed to clean the turkey for me.

Thanksgiving Day arrived. I cooked homemade pies the day before. Then the day of turkey, biscuits, homemade stuffing, corn, and green beans—not on a pizza, but in a bowl—and gravy. Food covered the entire table.

The American players and coaches showed up at the

designated time. The Venezuelans showed up a bit later, but they came. Their eyes bulged when they entered our apartment, seeing the buttery rolls, creamy corn, and basted turkey. They ate and left with full bellies.

The following week, many players began to share the names of their favorite restaurants or homemade food from their homes. One of the players asked us to go with him to his grandmother's house. He wanted to introduce us to her. We entered her open door with open hearts and a translation book. What an honor to be invited into his life and home.

When we seek connections, they can significantly impact our lives and others. Self-awareness of what makes us uncomfortable or self-conscious helps us stand firm in connecting.

The choice to connect with others inevitably fails if left to our feelings of comfort. We have to choose whom we serve, ourselves or God. We embrace the uncomfortable if we look at each interaction as a divine appointment the Lord has orchestrated.

★ ★ ★

BUT AS FOR ME

*"But as for me and my household,
we will serve the Lord."*

Joshua 24:15

For forty years, the Israelites traveled a complicated route through the desert. They didn't follow their leader, Moses. They refused to obey God and conquer the land. So they wandered with no direction. After Moses' death, Joshua became their leader. A brilliant military leader and a strong spiritual influence, his success came from his submission to God.

Joshua committed his life to obey God, even in the desert, with a bunch of whiny, disobedient friends. He told them in his final message how important it was to obey God. He challenged them to choose.

The time comes when we have to choose who or what will control us. The choice is ours. Will we allow God's divine appointments (encounters with people God desires to put in front of us), even if awkward and uncomfortable, to make us take risks? Will we deepen our connections with new friends in unusual conditions? Or will we allow fear to stifle our opportunities to create a new friend group with the potential to be more like family?

In taking a stand for the Lord, Joshua displayed his spiritual leadership. Regardless of what others decided, Joshua committed everything to God, willing to set the example of living by that decision. How we connect shows others our commitment to love others as Jesus loved us.

Making A Choice

When David and I began our adventure in baseball, we were not walking out our faith. We had good hearts and cared for others but didn't have what it took to surround ourselves with the people God intended us to love. We built emotional barriers, and anger roared at times.

Our hearts were forever changed when we committed our lives to the Lord. The emotional barriers we created from past relationships began to heal as we read the Bible and learned how to walk the walk Jesus invited us to.

We chose to put our egos aside. Our baseball life became more about including and supporting others. Our mission field grew from the coaches, players, and wives to the ticket takers, vendors, and grounds crew.

Peacemaking and encouragement became our anthem. Our compassion grew as we gained respect and trusted the people God gave us to love.

We chose to be generous with the love God poured into our lives by giving it freely to others. We decided to have fun in our baseball experiences, embracing each adventure.

Choosing Love

What is your choice? React to the situation you've found yourself in, or be proactive in building relationships?

When we react, our actions reveal our feelings. Feelings are never trustworthy and get us in trouble by overvaluing what our "gut" tells us. Reactive people are affected by the environment around them.

Our social environment can be a catalyst for a boomerang of feelings. When we are annoyed or affected by someone's behavior, we can return that attitude to them. Reactionary people base their relationship strength on others' behaviors. It allows others to control our connections.

Not everyone will like you. Nor will you like everyone. Not being fond of someone is no excuse for not loving them. Loving others is not an option. We are required to love others—God commands it.

To develop successful and loving relationships, we are responsible and response-able. We can respond rather than react. Enabling a response rather than a reaction releases the control of love from us to others.

Growing Connections

Initiating proactive responses means more than just taking the initiative. It means we are responsible for the growth of connections.

Having self-control before reacting to circumstances that make us stand on the outside and not take a risk in an uncomfortable situation is the basis of a proactive person.

Sometimes, our position in a group makes us feel like we don't want to step out and take a chance. These are the times the choice to serve the Lord where He has placed you override the feeling. So put away all hostility, deception, dishonesty, and comparison.

Let's not get crazy and think that if we feel the Holy Spirit telling us to run, we sit there. But when someone speaks a different language, and we are afraid to look dumb by pulling out our phones and loading a translation app, we must accept the awkward feeling and do it anyway.

A new mom shows up in the car line with a better car than ours, and we don't think we're good enough to welcome her to the school. A co-worker shows up ready to rock it, and we feel intimidated. A new player on a team, the new wife, or the new mom shows up, and they seem different than we are.

Choosing to make the most of our God appointments empowers us to seek connections. Being proactive determines how we serve the Lord, even if difficult. Embrace the uncomfortable.

What will you choose today? I pray you will decide to commit to building loving relationships. Toughening your skin as you commit to the process of growing. Embrace the uncomfortable.

★ ★ ★

FINAL OUT

Can I say how much I love you all? From the beginning of my idea about how we can grow in love for others until now, I've prayed for you. Because of God's great love for us, I can love each of you and enjoy it.

As we've moved through the four types of relationships and the Starting Nine Core Qualities, we've been growing in our ability to develop loving relationships.

Defining the types of relationships and their differences, the confusion of our connections has been identified and opened our hearts and minds to connect with each according to the type.

Not everyone will be on our team forever, but we must love them anyway. Treating an *Accidental Acquaintance* like there is potential to become *Forever Family* is loving someone who needs a boost.

We follow the command Jesus gives us to love one another. We become more aware of what God desires in our relationships. Love is uplifting and upholding.

With examples of my baseball life as a baseball wife relating to my baseball family, I believe we found ways to interact with others lovingly, even if baseball isn't your thing.

I have one question. Who's on your team? I hope this book has helped you define the connections, relieved you of the pressure to grow, and given you the freedom to deepen the maturing relationships.

Learning the four relationship types and the Starting Nine Core Qualities, we understand where boundaries are applicable and enforced to protect our hearts, minds, and souls. But we're also being challenged to step into connections even if they may never grow.

Like the final out of the game, this is the end of this experience. But today is the day to begin the work for what's to come.

Be confident that we can create and develop loving relationships with the distinctive types of connections as we apply the biblical principles behind the qualities. Take practical steps to grow with one another.

While we embrace the core qualities, we use them daily, stepping out and sharing sincere love without fear.

God wants to use us. He doesn't want it to be a complete sacrifice without joy. He desires us to dedicate our lives to fulfilling the command to love one another, glorifying Jesus in all we say and do, in response to His abundant love for us, and celebrating every opportunity.

★ ★ ★

LOVE DEEPLY FROM THE HEART

"Now that you have purified yourselves by obeying the truth
so that you have sincere love for each other,
love one another deeply, from the heart."

1 Peter 1:22

Sincere love involves selfless giving. God's love and forgiveness free us to take our eyes off ourselves and to meet others' needs.

By sacrificing His life, Christ showed that He loves us. Now we can love others by following His example and giving of ourselves sacrificially.

The apostle Peter wrote this letter to encourage believers who would likely face trials and persecution under Emperor Nero.

During most of the first century, Christians were hunted down and killed throughout the Roman empire. They could expect social and economic persecution from the Romans, the Jews, and their families. They would be misunderstood, harassed, and a few tortured or put to death.

Peter may have been writing to the new Christians. He wanted them to be warned of what lay ahead and to encourage and help them as they faced opposition. For today's readers, the theme of this letter is hope.

As we learn what God says about how to love one another, we are purified in the word. The scripture retrains our thinking. Our thinking transforms our actions.

Peter wants all believers to share sincere, brotherly love for each other. God sparked life in you to share that fire with others. The love Christ has filled us with isn't only to be shared with other believers but with all of humanity.

When others treat us poorly, we are to continue to love, despite the turmoil. We are God's servants and are called to be good at that because God commands it. Love one another and be kind.

Imagine what it will be like when we stand face-to-face with Jesus, and He says, "Well done! You loved others well."

CELEBRATE THE OPPORTUNITIES

Oh, the joy of how each quality shows love.

- *Selfless love* means seeing others' needs as more important than our wants.

- *Inclusive love* is going above and beyond to build connections with people we may never choose.

- *Supportive love* is helping others along the way with God's word and prayer.

- *Peacemaking love* means using God's love to create loving relationships, even when chaos reigns.

- *Encouraging love* helps stimulate confidence and hope by putting courage in another person's spirit.

- *Compassionate love* shows sympathy toward another's distress while having the desire to alleviate their pain.

- *Respectful love* cares enough about another person to consider how our actions impact them.

- *Trustworthy love* pours out dependable, reliable, and honest character.

- *Generous love* gives more affection and tenderness than is necessary.

Celebrate the opportunities God places in front of you. Take a chance to make friends and grow them into family. At the same time, continue to understand the connections that may never grow but deserve the intention of loving them while we are together.

It's hard to celebrate opportunities when we are busy or stressed. So we need to take a breath. Pause. And be intentional.

Welcome *Accidental Acquaintances* as if they've been *Forever Family* for a long time. Light up when you meet them. Our attitude expresses our heart. Recognize that we are more alike than we would think.

Continually be on the lookout for how to spread Christ's love. Who around us is in need? It's easier to help our *Kindred Spirits* and *Forever Family*, but we must show that same excitement to our *Social Circle* and *Accidental Acquaintances*.

An open invitation to each of the four relationships to spend quality time with them, no matter how much time we have together.

Despite the time, taking down the walls built between us and opening our hands to impact or be impacted by others allow us to grow loving connections.

Over time, evaluate the Starting Nine Core Qualities and the potential to grow when lacking. Only sometimes will we feel as if we are overflowing with love, but we must dig into the core qualities that come naturally while working on improving the ones we are weakest at sharing.

My friend, I pray for you as you read this book and embark on new opportunities to spread the love of Christ. As we build on the foundation of God's love by loving others, we spread the virtues of the Starting Nine Core Qualities, fulfilling God's command.

We create loving relationships as these core qualities become our daily habits. Celebrate the opportunities and take a risk. God will grow your *Forever Family*.

Celebrate God all day. Make it clear to others that you are full of God's love. Help them see Jesus through your actions.

I'm proud of you for finishing the book. But know this is not the end of our connection. I'm here for you, one and all. If I can help, let me know as we share God's love with others.

I pray you have been filled with courage, are ready to love others, and are prepared to impact the world as reliable and tender people. Love matters.

Now, let's have some fun! Wrap each other up in the over-pouring of love of Christ without holding back.

Baseball Family Study Questions

The Foundations of Four Relationships

1. What non-romantic relationship obstacles do you have that keep you from building loving relationships?
2. Who has stepped in the gap for you in your life? And what characteristic does that person have that helped you connect with them?
3. How is biblical love defined?
4. What new command does Jesus give in John 3:34-35?
5. In your own words, explain *Accidental Acquaintance*, *Social Circle*, *Kindred Spirit*, and *Forever Family*. Can you identify one person in each group you have connected with?

The Starting Nine Core Qualities

1. What do you most want to learn about building loving relationships regarding the Starting Nine Core Qualities?
2. What keeps you from connecting with others?
3. Which core quality do you feel you have the most strength in? The least?
4. Write a prayer in expectation of what God will do in your life regarding your relationships and strengthening the core qualities.

5. How do you define success? What would you expect success to look like in your life after reading *Baseball Family*?

Selflessness

1. How do you define *selflessness* in your own words? What is selfless love?
2. How do you feel when you think of selflessness?
3. Write Philippians 2:3 in your own words.
4. What does spiritual unity mean to you?
5. Write three ways to show selflessness to *Accidental Acquaintances*, *Social Circles*, *Kindred Spirits*, and *Forever Family*.

Inclusion

1. Write one experience of feeling like an outsider.
2. Who is one person who has included you? What characteristics of inclusion did they show?
3. What does being devoted to and honoring others above yourself mean to you?
4. What example of kindness and love is in Jesus' relationship with His disciples in John 13:1-12?
5. Write three examples of how you can include others for each of the four relationships: *Accidental Acquaintances*, *Social Circles*, *Kindred Spirits*, and *Forever Family*.

Supportive

1. How or when has someone supported you?
2. How have you been unfairly judged as a person? How have you unfairly judged another person?
3. What characteristics do you see in Elijah and Elisha's relationship?
4. Read Matthew 9:1-8. Where do you find the strength to support others as these friends did for the paralyzed man?

5. Write three ways you can show supportive love to others in each of the four relationships: *Accidental Acquaintances, Social Circles, Kindred Spirits,* and *Forever Family.*

Peacemaker

1. What does being a peacemaker mean to you?
2. What tactics can help redirect glory thieves?
3. What does *shalom* mean?
4. How can we seek peace and pursue it?
5. Write three ways to show peacemaking love to each of the four relationships: *Accidental Acquaintances, Social Circles, Kindred Spirits,* and *Forever Family.*

Encouraging

1. What does it mean to be an encourager?
2. Explain a life-enriching relationship you've had.
3. What do you need to avoid when being an encourager? What are examples of building each other up?
4. What qualities do you see in Barnabas, Son of Encouragement, in Acts 9:26-31?
5. Write three ways to encourage each relationship: *Accidental Acquaintances, Social Circles, Kindred Spirits,* and *Forever Family.*

Compassionate

1. Have you had a relationship you've checked off as too hard? List the things that made it hard.
2. What does giving and receiving forgiveness mean to you?
3. Read Matthew 9: 27-38. How did Jesus show compassion for the physical and spiritual needs of the people He encountered?
4. What does it mean to be a compassionate Christian?

5. Write three ways to show compassion to each of our *Accidental Acquaintances, Social Circles, Kindred Spirits,* and *Forever Family.*

Respectful

1. How do you define the quality of being respectful? Disrespectful?
2. When have you lacked self-respect? How did you build it back?
3. Do you believe respect must be earned or given?
4. Jesus taught the Sermon on the Mount in Matthew 7. Read Matthew 7. Write Matthew 7:12 in your own words.
5. Write three ways to be an advocate of Christ by being respectful to each of the four relationships: *Accidental Acquaintances, Social Circles, Kindred Spirits,* and *Forever Family.*

Trustworthy

1. What experience has caused you to lose trust in someone?
2. What are the qualities of someone you trust?
3. What does Paul say to Titus in Titus 2:6-8 about being trustworthy?
4. What does God entrust to us, and how are we to handle it?
5. Write three ways to be trustworthy for our *Accidental Acquaintances, Social Circles, Kindred Spirits,* and *Forever Family.*

Generous

1. Where does a generous spirit begin?
2. What are some examples of giving other than money?
3. What does Paul say about serving humbly in love?

4. What are the fruit of the Spirit? Write how you define each.

5. Write three ways to be openhanded to each of our *Accidental Acquaintances*, *Social Circles*, *Kindred Spirits*, and *Forever Family*.

Significant Impact

1. What makes you uncomfortable when connecting with others?
2. Explain some of God's divine appointments in your life.
3. Will you choose to serve God by building loving relationships? What is your first step?
4. Define *response-able* in your own words.
5. How can you make the most of your God appointments?

Final Out

1. What are some of the baseball examples that helped you understand the Starting Nine Core Qualities?
2. What are some baseball examples you remember that helped you understand the four relationships?
3. How do you describe the sincere brotherly love Peter talks about in 1 Peter 1:22?
4. Rewrite each of the Starting Nine Core Qualities that describe love in your own words.
5. Write a note to yourself describing how you exemplify the Starting Nine Core Qualities.

Love Deeply from the Heart

1. Are there things still standing in the way of you being able to love others? List them.
2. Are there people who are a stumbling block for you to love them freely? List them.

3. Begin to work on the reasons holding you back by researching scripture that will help.
4. How do you define "brotherly love"?
5. How do you plan to love others so you hear Jesus say, "Well done! You loved others well"?

Celebrate the Opportunities

1. Make a list of ways you can connect with others.
2. Invite someone new for coffee. Gather some people to celebrate the life we live together.
3. Name a few people you are connecting with who you feel can grow into a deeper relationship.
4. Throw some confetti!
5. I'm here for you. If I can help, let me know.

Baseball Family Quotes

"God's faithfulness in the game is the one thing I learned over the years. The many teams, organizations, and levels you can be with can be overwhelming. God and His faithfulness never fail despite the different people we interact with during all those times and changes.

Leaning into God and asking me to pray for others was such an easy thing for me because of His faithfulness. I recognize this new place they are walking into, and God asks me to pray. My statement of faith is to love others and let them know God is a foundation they'll need if they want to have a good go in the field God has called us to."

Renette Manuel
Wife of Jerry, Former Chicago White Sox Manager and Founder of the Jerry Manuel Foundation

"My husband played the game for many years. I learned very quickly that baseball mimics life. Adversity is always around the corner. Words of sincere encouragement were precious to my husband. Throughout his career, I made a conscious effort to honor Matt through words of encouragement. I wanted him to know, for certain, that his value in our home extended past his success on the baseball field. We are so proud of all that he accomplished, but how my guy loves Jesus anchored our family. I never missed an opportunity to encourage him in the faith and tell him how much I appreciate his leadership in our home."

Leslee Holliday
Director of Women's Ministry with Pro Athletes Outreach
Wife of Matt, Former Player with Colorado Rockies,
Oakland Athletics, St. Louis Cardinals, New York Yankees
Mother of Jackson Holliday, Current Player with
Baltimore Orioles

"In May 2019, my husband was traded to the Pittsburgh Pirates. We'd been with the same organization for six years and were on our third team in less than two months. I showed up weary and afraid to get settled. I was overwhelmed trying to get our two kids under three settled on a new team and in a new city once again.

At one of my first Pirates Bible studies, I opened up about how I was scared to get settled and fully embrace being in Pittsburgh because I knew we'd get traded again as soon as I did.

The girls encouraged me to 'unpack' physically and emotionally. I knew God was telling me I needed to be fully there no matter how long it was. He had us in Pittsburgh for a reason, and I needed to let my walls down and embrace that.

A few weeks later, we met 'our people.' We've met many people we love in baseball, but this friendship immediately felt different. They are the kind of friends that are more like family. And if I had kept my walls up out of fear, I would have missed out on finding our people.

I'm so thankful I took down my walls and embraced the uncomfortable. God knew what He was doing. Sometimes we must embrace the awkward and new to see what He has for us."

Martha Kate Stratton
Wife of Chris Stratton, MLB Pitcher, 2023 World Series Champion, Texas Rangers

"My sister friends may not be perfect, they have flaws like everyone else, although I prefer to enjoy their virtues. What I love most about them is the way they help me straighten up when they see me bent over and not to mention when they see me without strength. I think they have a secret book on how to push me to be better every day. God has been good with me." *(translated from Spanish)*

Noelia Brazoban
1988-2020
Wife of Starling Marte, MLB Player

"'I researched it, you can eat all the cactus you want, and it won't raise your blood sugar.' I heard this when being handed a Tupperware full of cactus salsa.

I had told the wives on the team that I had just failed my gestational diabetes test while pregnant with my third baby. Throughout my husband's baseball career, generosity and being humbly served went hand in hand. From weddings to baby showers and the mundane—this level of support was always felt by my baseball family.

By starting the nonprofit *The Prom Series,* I have first-hand seen and felt the generosity of baseball women. They have welcomed the idea of serving teens in foster care and have run with it. Every summer, they have provided thousands of back-to-school outfits for teens in foster care. The thought they put behind every outfit they send is just amazing. I am forever grateful for them serving a community in need so well."

Tori Murphy
Founder of *The Prom Series*
Wife of Daniel Murphy, MLB Player, 2008-2020
Mom of Four

"As crowded as baseball stadiums get on a game day, they can be a lonely place for a baseball wife. We can always spot 'one of us' from a mile away. She's sitting alone, sunglasses on, phone in hand, with gorgeous hair. I swear, even their messy buns are beautiful! One of the most valuable lessons I've learned as a baseball wife came from being that girl alone in the stands. I was sitting at a game in the Dominican Republic when a woman sat beside me and asked me, '¿Cómo te llamas?' (What is your name?) I knew enough Spanish to say, 'Jessica, pero no hablo mucho Español.' I assumed that would be the end of that, and I'd be left by myself again.

She quickly pulled out her phone and handed me the Google Translate app. On it, she had typed out into translation for me, 'That's okay; we are still friends.' She smiled at me, patted my thigh, and sat with me for the rest of the game.

By the time I ended my visit to my husband, I had new friends, a new nickname, and a new understanding of the value of inclusion. Inclusion doesn't have a language barrier. It's a smile, a gesture, the use of an app, or simply an invitation not to sit alone. The love I felt through this small act by a woman in a foreign country perfectly reflected the love of Christ. Unconditional, without limits, and all-inclusive."

Jessica Anderson
Wife to Johnny Anderson, Former Player
Mom to Cooper
Baseball Chapel Representative

"Merriam-Webster defines the adjective trustworthy as worthy of confidence: DEPENDABLE. That is exactly how the baseball community has been. Dependable! My husband Brad and I have been the Chaplains for the Pittsburgh Pirates for over 20 years. Over the years, we have seen players/coaches and their significant others come and go. We are always sad when they leave, thinking there will never be another player/coach as dependable as they are, but the Lord continues to provide reliable, trustworthy people in their place. It truly is amazing. I thought it was a Pittsburgh Pirates phenomenon, but now I believe it is this family called Baseball. They are good, God-fearing folks that we love and can depend on no matter what!

I became a chaplain for an MLB team with fear and trembling, thinking there was no way I could ever trust or depend on women in baseball. I was wrong! These ladies are some of the most dependable women I know. They keep confidence and care for others; when they commit, they are committed for life. Baseball sisters are the absolute best!"

Beth Henderson
Baseball Chapel Women's Leader for Pittsburgh Pirates
Wife of Brad Henderson, President of Pittsburgh
Kids Foundation and Baseball Chapel Chaplain for
Pittsburgh Pirates

"When I think of our baseball life, community is at the forefront of it all. God truly has blessed us beyond what we ever could've imagined, and we both felt a strong calling to give back to our community and start our non-profit, The Alonso Foundation. What started as a tug on our hearts in 2020 has blossomed into what we believe to be our lifetime vocation. We know that someday his baseball career will end, and we felt it was important to find something we are passionate about to continue long after he retires from the game. Serving others has brought us an immense amount of joy. We have met some of the most incredible people through our outreach and learned much from them. Someone that has been our inspiration is Roberto Clemente, a hall-of-fame baseball player who is not only known for what he accomplished on the field but even more widely known for his humanitarian efforts. Roberto is the perfect example that simply being good to others is the best legacy to leave."

Haley Alonso
Wife of Pete Alonso, MLB Player

Baseball Glossary

At Bat: A player's turn to attempt to hit the ball and reach a base.

Away Team: The team visiting another team's ballpark.

Away Game: A game played on an opposing team's field.

Backup Plays: When a player intentionally goes behind another player who is attempting to field the ball, in case they misplay it.

Base: One of the three spots on the infield that a baserunner must touch to score a run.

Baseball Diamond: The shape of the baseball field which is covered in grass and dirt.

Baseball Family: The people in our baseball community.

Baseball Game: Nine innings, twenty-seven outs, three outs when one team hits in the top of the inning and three outs when the other team hits in the bottom of the inning.

Basemen: The baseball players who are responsible for the defensive positions at first, second, and/or third base.

Batterymates: The catcher and pitcher who are paired together in a game.

Bunt: When a ball is not swung at but is intentionally met with the bat and tapped slowly within the infield.

Call Off: When a player tells another player he can make the play, usually in a fly ball situation.

Corner Outfielders: Left and right fielders.

Defense: When the team is positioned in the field attempting to prevent the offense from reaching base and scoring runs.

Defense Strategy: The primary object of the defense to prevent the offense from getting on base and scoring runs.

Dribble Hit: When a batter attempts to hit the ball, but, unintentionally, it softly bounces on the infield.

Field the Ball: When a ball is in play on the ground and a player makes a play.

Fly Ball: A ball in the air to the outfield that a player attempts to catch.

Game Plan: A carefully thought-out strategy for how to win the game to be played.

Home Game: A game played on the team's field.

Home Team: The team that is hosting the game. They play defense in the top of an inning and offense in the bottom of an inning.

Hits: When a player makes contact with the bat on the ball and it falls into fair territory on the field.

In-Between Innings: When the teams change places on the field from offense to defense, or defense to offense, after three outs are made.

Infield: The portion of the baseball field where most of the plays are made. It is made up of dirt where the catcher and the first, second, and third basemen, along with the shortstop, cover. It also includes the pitcher's mound.

Infielders: First, second, and third basemen and the shortstop.

Infield Fly: A ball in the air in the infield that an infielder or catcher attempts to catch.

Infield Fly Ball: A fair fly ball that can be caught by an infielder with ordinary effort when first and second, or first, second, and third bases are occupied before there are two outs.

Inning: The portion of the baseball game when teams alternate on offense and defense and in which there are three outs for each team.

Mound: The slight elevation where the pitcher stands.

Mound Visit: When one or more members of a baseball team go to the mound to visit the pitcher.

Offense: When a team is hitting and scoring runs.

Offense Strategy: Batters attempting to hit the ball, get on base, and score more runs than the opposing team.

Off-Season: The time between the last game played and spring training.

Outfield: The grass portion of the field beyond the infield and in front of the fence/wall that is covered by the outfielders.

Outfielders: The three players in right, center, and left, farthest from the batter.

Plays: The effort attempted and/or accomplished by a defensive player.

Runners: Players of the team at bat who make it to a base without getting an out.

Season: The time in which 162 baseball games are played in 187 days. 81 at home. 81 away.

Shorten Swing: When a batter doesn't make a complete swing of the bat.

Sign: A nonverbal form of communication between coaches and players or between players.

Spring Training: The preseason time in which teams work out and play exhibition games for approximately six weeks.

Starting Pitcher: The pitcher that begins the game against the opposing team on offense.

Strikeout: When a pitcher throws any combination of three swinging or looking strikes to a hitter.

Winter Ball: Baseball played during the off-season in countries outside the United States.

Endnotes

Rick Warren. *The Purpose Driven Life: What on Earth Am I Here For?* Grand Rapids: Zondervan, 2012.

"Diversity in MLB Continues to Expand, on Field and off." MLB.com. Last modified April 13, 2022. https://www.mlb.com/news/diversity-in-mlb-expanding.

"Definition of ENCOURAGE." Merriam-Webster: America's Most Trusted Dictionary. Last modified 12, 2023. https://www.merriam-webster.com/dictionary/encourage.

Baseball Chapel. Accessed July 25, 2023. https://baseball-chapel.org/.

Pro Athletes Outreach. Accessed July 25, 2023. https://pao.org.

"How About Sponsoring a Child in Poverty Today?" Sponsor Children in Need for Holistic Child Development. https://www.compassion.com/sponsor_a_child/?utm_source=purl&utm_medium=purl&utm_campaign=billie-jauss-657911&referer=657911.

Acknowledgments

Thank you to my hubby, David, who dragged me into this crazy life. Thank you for loving me well as we both found our footing.

To my baseball boys, who I birthed, DJ, Charley, and Will. Remember to walk through life understanding that love never fails to build healthy relationships.

To my baseball girls, we've lived through many wins, losses, travel, packing, moving, kids, parents, and interesting relationships. Thank you for sharing life with me.

To my baseball girls who are marrying into the Jauss family. Love conquers all. Thank you for loving my boys well.

To my baseball boys given to me in the baseball world, thanks for receiving the hugs even after a tough game.

To my Dream Team of Prayer Warriors: Bridgett, Courtney, Debi, Fran, Gail, Ingrid, Jan, Jeannine, Rene, Valerie, and Wendy. For most of you, this is OUR third book. We've gone to battle on our knees together in prayer for this book, and I am so thankful for you.

To the baseball women who shared in the book. Renette, Leslee, Martha Kate, Tori, Jessica, Beth, and Haley keep leaving that legacy of loving one another with each encounter you have! Thank you for sharing a little of your heart. And to

Noelia, who left an indelible marking of love on my heart, rest my friend.

To Michelle Medlock Adams. Thank you for talking through my concerns and worries regarding writing about baseball. I came to you for an out, and you encouraged me to hit a home run. Thank you for your wisdom.

To Terry Whalin, who taught me how to write a book proposal in *Book Proposals that Sell*. From the words of your book to your friendship and encouragement now, I thank you. You are a treasure.

To Cindy Sproles, thank you for your meticulous reading, editing, and advice, again.

To Gail Mills, you've been with me since the beginning. I thank you for your commitment to making my writing better each time.

To those who endorsed the book, I thank you for your honest feedback and encouragement.

To my book launch team…you rock! Together, we can make a difference for the kingdom.

To the editors who made this book better, you are talented beyond measure. Thank you!

End Game Press, Victoria Duerstock. What a great experience with a publishing house that cares about the product and the author, but mostly the readers. I appreciate your commitment.

★ ★ ★

ABOUT THE AUTHOR

Billie Jauss is the author of *Making Room: Doing Less So God Can Do More* and *Distraction Detox*. Billie is a national speaker and the host of The Family Room podcast. Billie and Dave, a Major League Baseball coach, spend the summers chasing baseball and the off-season in southwest Florida.